1-800 -9753.1⁰⁰

MW00986117

The Messianic Seal
of the
Jerusalem Church
First Edition

**Reuven Efraim Schmalz
And Raymond Robert Fischer**

Olim Publications
P.O. Box 2111, Tiberias, Israel

Cover Picture: The Messianic Seal of the Jerusalem Church pointing down to the copper domed upper room above the Tomb of David on Mount Zion

© 1999 by Olim Creative Products (1994) Ltd.
P.O. Box 2111, Tiberias, Israel

ISBN 965-222-962-8

*Unless otherwise noted, scripture quotations are from the New King James Version of the Holy Bible.
Copyright © 1979, 1980, 1982.
Used by permission of Thomas Nelson, Inc.*

Printed in Israel

TABLE OF CONTENTS

Foreword

The rediscovery of the first century Judeo-Christian synagogue on Mount Zion has been both the most exciting and challenging experience of our lives; exciting, because the Messianic Seal of the Jerusalem Church, re-emerged after nearly 2,000 years of burial, carries with it implications that, we believe, can literally change the world; challenging, because we have, in our separate research, "unearthed" an enormous amount of information, some entirely historical, some more biblically oriented.

The challenge was how to best present Reuven's decidedly historical information, an incredibly interesting story in itself, as a solid background for Bob's (R.R. Fischer's) more biblically oriented interpretation and commentary. After testing several approaches, we determined to present this book in two parts: Part One, an entirely historical presentation of the events spanning several centuries, leading up to the emergence of the Nazarene Sect of Judaism and ultimately, to the Jerusalem Church the Nazarenes established on Mount Zion; Part Two, a biblical interpretation of the Messianic Seal and a suggestion regarding its contemporary implications.

This entirely Jewish "Mother Church" was the genesis of all subsequent ecclesiastical Christianity, until the present day, when more than two billion adherents world-wide can look to the "Stump of Jesse" astride the very throne of King David on Mount Zion from which both Jesus and the church "sprouted" forth.

Although it was carved and painted by the hands of the very first believers, perhaps even by one or more of the twelve apostles themselves, we believe the Messianic Seal proclaims several monumentally important messages, all of them just as applicable today as they were when they were first scribed.

It is our profound hope and expectation that these messages of the Messianic Seal of the Jerusalem Church will strike at the very roots and foundations of the several man-made barriers that have, over the centuries, separated Jew from Jew, and Jew from Gentile, while they have simultaneously spawned the horrors of anti-Semitism.

May there also evolve from all this, a new sense of unity as the church returns to Mount Zion, and together, Jewish and Gentile believers alike can finally find the common Jewish roots of their faith.

RES and RRF

Preface

On Friday, February 5, 1999, we were ushered by a uniformed maid into Ludwig Schneider's voluminous library in the Schneider residence in Jerusalem.

Ludwig Schneider is a man with a powerful, classic German face, a bright smile, and piercing, sky blue eyes. His obvious vitality and almost boyish manner seem somehow to conflict with his easy flowing Germanesque formality, belying his 58 years.

Within moments we were holding the first of the eight awesome relics in our hands—a brick size rectangle of local marble, adorned with an etched version of the ancient symbol, and words in archaic Aramaic letters proclaiming: "For the oil of the Spirit." An interesting difference in this piece from the others: a tiny etched cross formed the fish's eye.

One of the other remarkable pieces was a small ceramic vial, appearing like it could well have been used to hold anointing oil, and originally have been placed upon the "stand for anointing oil." Both of these, like all of the artifacts, were found in the same place, in a grotto adjacent to the upper room, which is located directly astride the ancient and revered tomb of King David.

Another piece is the remains of a small marble pillar, and the others, a small ceremonial oil lamp and an assortment of various size pottery shards with painted versions of the symbol. All of these artifacts are etched, embossed or painted with renditions of the same three-part symbol of menorah, star of David and fish.

All of the pieces were unquestionably authentic to even an amateur eye. To Reuven, a self-trained historian and archeologist, sculptor, and a long-time student of the early church and first century history in general, these pieces were clearly genuine.

Finally, after we both, with awe, had carefully examined each of the eight pieces, Ludwig's wife served us Turkish coffee which we sipped as Ludwig told his tantalizing story:

"In 1990," Ludwig began in good English, flavored with a delightful old world sounding German accent, "I became acquainted with Tech

iv

Oteeoos, a Greek Orthodox monk in his nineties who lived by himself in an obscure, dank and foul smelling, small building in the Old City of Jerusalem. I was drawn to the ancient monk whom I visited several times. I kept my distance until he could emerge into the fresh air. The human stench of the dwelling kept me from exploring its interior.

"One day," Ludwig continued, " I believe it was on my third visit, Tech Oteeoos showed me, to my absolute amazement, several ancient artifacts which he had excavated at a nearby site, in the vicinity of the building traditionally known as the original church founded by James the Just, the brother of Jesus. The central feature of each piece was a hand-executed rendition of the symbol, either etched into or painted upon the surface.

"Needless to say, I was fascinated by both the symbol and its obvious significance. It was clear to me that God Himself had laid before me a long-forgotten testimony informing the world about the true roots of the Church.

"Several visits later, the old monk finally lured me into the interior of his foul smelling dwelling. It was there that I saw for the first time his collection of about 30 to 40 beautiful and varied pieces, all bearing the three-part symbol. As I stared at this treasure in wonder, my host carefully selected eight of the pieces which he later,during a subsequent visit, presented to me as a gift. On this occasion, I excitedly photographed the eight artifacts which had been set aside for me.

"But an even greater gift from this dear messenger of God lay in store for me. During a subsequent visit, after he had, as usual, devoured my chocolate bar gift, he took me by the hand and led me to the nearby site where he had personally excavated his entire collection. This special place was an obviously very old Jewish mikva located near the Tomb of David.

"After we had climbed over an unimposing fence, the old man led me down the traditional seven cosmic stairs leading to the place used for ceremonial cleansing. We proceeded past this place, and entered a catacomb that continued on into the quickly fading light. After what seemed like a short distance, just before the first bend, my ancient monk friend and benefactor was excitedly pointing out his special gift to me on one of the walls, a perfect rendition of the three-part symbol etched into the stone.

"In my initial excitement, I rushed back to the priests of the monastery to report this incredible find. I was shocked by the audience I received. They rebuffed me, refused to answer my questions about the "Seal" and locked me outside the monastery gate.

"I was overwhelmed by the great significance of the find, and its meaning to the Church and the entire world," Ludwig continued, "and I determined with confidence, that I should bring these pieces to the attention of the Israel Museum, so they, in turn, could promulgate their incredible message to the world. Thus I called the curator of the museum and made an appointment.

"The curator was most friendly, even gracious. I was ushered into his office with the pictures of the eight pieces which he examined with careful and studied interest. He then told me, matter of factly that the museum already had seen other artifacts with this very same three-part symbol that had come to them from other sources which he did not specify. The curator assured me that the museum had firm plans to have a special exhibition of these artifacts and their unique symbol, and that they would make an announcement regarding them to the world press in the near future. This was in 1990. Quite frankly, I am not surprised that these artifacts or the three-part symbol with which they are adorned have as yet—as far as I know, never emerged, nor has any information about them. Israeli officialdom, perhaps, was afraid of what the world might think if the truth became known: the early church was Jewish, and the original believers in Jesus were Jews.

"You can't imagine my frustration over this seeming suppression, but even more, my sorrow when I returned for a somewhat delayed visit to my dear benefactor Tech Oteeoos. Tearfully, I learned that he had died, and irrespective of his earlier promise that the rest of the pieces were to be mine, his dwelling had been completely emptied, and all of his remaining treasure had vanished.

"Despite the passage of years, I couldn't stop thinking about the importance of the symbol and the need to present it to the world. It was thus in 1996 that I opened a small gift shop in the Old City where I sold traditional tourist gift items, to which I added several products bearing a simple artist's rendition of the ancient symbol.

"Within days, I was threatened by Orthodox Rabbis who insisted that I remove these 'evil, heathen' objects from my shop. By now, although none had any idea about the profound significance of their purchases, tourists had begun to enthusiastically buy my symbol adorned souvenirs in sufficient quantity to entice my nearby competitor shops (some owned by orthodox Jews) to produce and offer for sale, copies of my unique products.

"This unfriendly competition wasn't to last long. When I refused to remove these items from my shop, the orthodox gathered outside in large numbers and stoned the place, breaking my windows: not once, but several times. I finally gave up, and closed my shop less than a year after it had been opened, taking little satisfaction from the fact that the other shops had also soon removed the symbol-carrying products from their own shelves. Presumably, between the combined efforts of the Israel Museum and the orthodox rabbis, the precious symbol proclaiming the true origins of the Church had vanished from public view.

"My earnest prayer," Ludwig concluded, "is that the truth about the Jewish origins of the Christian Church will be made known throughout the world so that all might know: Jesus was a Jew, the early (first century) church in Jerusalem was attended exclusively by a sect of Essene Jews who had accepted Jesus as their Messiah, and the entire church in the world today has been built upon this precious Jewish foundation."

RES and RRF

Part One

THE MESSIANIC SEAL OF THE JERUSALEM CHURCH

The Rediscovery of the First Century Sectarian Center of James the Just, the Apostles, and the Nazarenes on the Throne of David, Mount Zion, Jerusalem

By
Reuven Efraim Schmalz

Author's Note

Some of my friends and colleagues, both Jewish and Christian, who, for editorial, promotional, or other professional reasons have read my manuscript, have asked me what were my intentions in presenting this work.

For some, this was a religiously loaded question to which I must give a clear response.

Although I have documented this discovery essentially for the Christian reader, deeming it especially pertinent now, at the dawn of the third millennium, I have taken pains to express myself exclusively in secular, historical tones. My intention has been to present the current conclusions of a twenty-five year study in a manner that is as religiously unbiased as humanly possible. My quest has been for historical truth, and that alone.

It is my intention to follow-up this synopsized work, as time permits, with a full, book length exposition of my research. There is much of this incredible story that remains to be told.

My purpose is not to propagate any religious dogma or doctrine, but to turn the page on a lost chapter in history, to put down the lie of anti-Semitism, and to break down the walls of prejudice between man and man to the edification of all. As always, mankind can only profit from being better informed.

R.E.S.

Introduction

My interest in this archeological find is decidedly historical. A lifetime private historical student, nearly all of my "free" or "hobby" time has been spent in this pursuit (my occupation is professional artist). The subject of my choice is late Second Temple Messianism. In my opinion, this period from approximately 200 BCE to 300 CE[1], is probably the most dynamic and volatile time in the history of the world.

In this period, acute messianism arose and took the world by storm. In two tremendously bloody uprisings, the tiny nation of Judah, which held the land bridge between the continents,[2] rocked the mighty Roman Empire to its very core.

When the smoke cleared in the fourth century, the age old pantheon of pagan gods had fallen to dust at the feet of the world wandering Jew, Paul. In one way of thinking, it was Judea that had conquered the Empire and not visa versa.

In 313, Christianity became the official religion of the Roman Empire. In these few, short centuries, the world was forever, dramatically changed. A new, world-wide culture was born, which has lasted up to this modern day.

After destroying Judea, massacring and enslaving many of its citizens, this mighty Empire would, within a mere 300 years from the time of Jesus, adopt a messianic form of the very God that it had most ruthlessly tried to destroy.

Even more absurd, the deposed "People of the Book" would then be relentlessly persecuted over a period of nearly 2,000 years, through pogroms, expulsions from occupational guilds, ghettoizations, blood libels, laws forbidding access to higher education or political office, expulsions, burning at the stake, crusades, the slaughter of entire communities, and forced conversions. Capped off with the Holocaust of Annihilation, this calamity was served to the tiny Jewish nation in the name of its own God.

---

[1] To the end of the Messianic Revolt when the Empire adopted Christianity.
[2] The King's Highway between Europe, Asia and Africa. Israel actually sits upon its own continent-like piece of the earth's crust west of the Syrian-African rift valley. This valley is the deepest and the longest dry land crack in the earth's surface caused by some prehistoric cataclysm. The whole valley, from the Galilee to below the Dead Sea, was once literally a "Lake of Fire," where the earth opened her mouth (Sodom and Gomorra).

Having said this, the saga begins.

The Backdrop

Alexander the Macedonian, surnamed the "Great," had pushed his armies across most of the then known world, conquering nation after nation and planting advanced Hellenistic Greek centers in his wake. Upon his untimely death, Alexander's empire was divided between his generals. In Alexandria, Egypt, the Ptolemies ruled, and in Syria and the Levant, power fell to the Seleucids.

In 173 BCE, Antiochus Epiphanius, the Seleucid king, performed the misdeed that, although barely noticed by historians, sparked the messianic revolt that would rise to a raging inferno and engulf the whole world. He deposed Onias III, the reigning hereditary High Priest of the House of Zadok. This was the anointed[3] of the Lord whose sacred duty it was to teach the nation the Law of God and stand before the mercy seat between the cherubim to receive atonement for his people.

The House of Zadok, appointed to the High Priestly office in perpetuity by David, and then by Solomon at the dedication of the First Temple, was in a state of debilitating shock. If this were not enough, Epiphanius proceeded to sell the holy office to the highest bidder: a non Zadokite priest.

The High Priestly office under the anointment of *YHWH*[4] was forbidden to any other son of Aaron[5] Any other impostor would be considered illegitimate,[6] and the Temple over which he presided, profaned.

---

[3] Hebrew-messiah

[4] *YHWH* is the only God among the Deities of the ancient world that had no earthly or describable image. The Tetragrammaton, also unlike the names of the pagan gods, is not a title or description of some power, rulership or deity. The ineffable name, in fact, is not a noun, but a verb, or verb intransitive expressing ultimate infinity. Contrary to the insistence of some, that the true and only pronunciation of the name is *YAHWEH*, seeing that this name connotes concept rather than title, the various verb spelling's throughout the Hebrew Bible include *EH HE YEH, YAHUWAH, YAHU, YEHO, YA, YE, YO,* etc. My two youngest children are variously named *Rinatya* (Joy or Song of Ya) and *Shmariyahu*, (*Yahu* has watched over me). The Name connotes existence: past, present, and future. In the great "I AM" verse (Exodus 3:13-15), God proclaims His name *EH HE YE*: (in the process of being). "This is my name forever, and this is my memorial to all generations." This name (concept) thus

10

Soon after this, Epiphanius proceeded to cancel the High Priestly office entirely and outlawed, under the penalty of death, the practice of the Jewish religion. Epiphanius, in June 168 BCE, desecrated the Temple in Jerusalem, offering swine's flesh upon the altar. Setting up an idol of Jupiter Olympius, he dedicated the Temple to this pagan deity.[7]

These deeds by Antiochus IV Epiphanius: the deposing of the High Priestly line of Zadok, the desecration of the Temple of *YHWH*, and the outlawing of Judaism struck a reverberating blow to the foundations of the ancient Hebraic nation and sacred culture.

Onias[8], and the faithful with him, spirited away to Leontopolis Egypt, where, by permission of the Ptolemaic authorities, he was given license to build a rival temple to *YHWH*. Here, those faithful of the archaic school could then offer their pure libations.[9]

After the Temple in Jerusalem had been profaned, a swine sacrificed upon the altar and an image of Zeus set up in its holy precincts, an old priest from the village of Modi'in rose to the challenge. Slaying a heretic Jew and a servant of the king, he took to the Judean Hills with his sons. Boldly, he called all those to gather to him who would be faithful Israelites and not bend at the knee to pagan Hellenism and to idols. Mattathias and his sons after him brought down their swords upon the Greeks. Driving out the Seleucids in a whirlwind gorilla war, the Maccabees took back the Temple and established their sovereignty in the land of Israel for a short period. They cleansed the Temple and rededicated the sacrifices on the first Festival of Hanukkah.

---

connotes the very ultimate, all-encompassing and infinite essence of existence itself in the continuing process of being. In many of the Dead Sea Scrolls, the sacred name is scribed in the original archaic Proto Hebrew script, and not in the new for the time Aramaic script of the text. This name was so sacred to the sect as not to be transliterated from the original Semitic script.

[5] Ezekiel 40:46, 43:19, 44:15. There existed a hierarchy of priestly families, each descended from a separate line of Aaron.

[6] 2Macc. 4:25

[7] This is the "abomination of Desolation" spoken of by the prophet Daniel (11:31).

[8] Josephus gives contradicting accounts as to whether this was Onias III or his son and successor to the High Priesthood, OniasIV. In one account, Onias III was murdered by Menaleos, the usurper High Priest near Antioch in Syria. This agrees with Maccabees and is therefore probably the correct account. Some commentators see Onias as the personage of the "Teacher of Righteousness," and Menaleos as the "Wicked Priest" of the Dead Sea Scrolls.

[9] This temple to *YHWH* in Leontopolis continued until after the fall of the Jerusalem Temple. It was   closed by Vespasian in 73 CE. (JOS., WAR 7:433-646) This Temple operated for over 240 years, longer than the lifetime of the United States of America.

The Plot Thickens

The Maccabees are remembered in Jewish history as national heroes. What again is barely noticed by historians, is that in two infamous acts, these "heroes" caused havoc and division in the nation and set the pace for the coming destruction and 2000 year exile.

In 152 BCE, Jonathan[10] the Maccabean took the High Priestly office to himself, and in the early years of his successor, Simeon,[11] the High Priesthood transferred irrevocably from the Zadokites to the Hasmoneans (Maccabees).[12] Considered impostors and usurpers by the Zadokites, the Hasmonean High Priests were counted as illegitimate, and their offerings and the very Temple itself profaned.

Delegitmatized and persecuted by the Hasmonean priesthood, the priests of the line of Zadok removed to the wilderness of Damascus along with an exodus of their followers. Thus was born the sect of the Essenes.

Banished, and left without any foreseeable hope of gaining back their rightful holy seat from the now increasingly Hellenized[13] Hasmoneans, the Essenes set up a community hailing the prophetic banner of Isaiah 40:3; i.e., "and these shall become a community in Israel according to these rules, they shall separate themselves from the dwellings of the people of lawlessness, to go into the wilderness and prepare there the way of the Lord as it is written: 'In the wilderness prepare you the way of the Lord'"[14] These were the first in Israel who waited upon the Kingdom of God.

In 1896, Solomon Schecter of Cambridge was handed manuscripts brought from the genizah of the ancient Karaite[15] synagogue of Cairo.

---

[10] In Epiphanes, Jonathan and Simeon, the concept of "Anti-Christ" (false anointed) was probably born.

[11] This is approximately the time that Josephus informs us (if we take 200 years as a rounded number), the Urim and Thumim ceased to answer God's oracle upon the breastplates of the High Priest. The Urim no longer shone, JOS., ANT. III, VIII: 4. This breastplate, ironically, was called the "Essene."

[12] The Hasmoneans belonged to the Jehoiarib Division of Priests, not eligible for the High Priestly office.

[13] The Maccabees who originally arose in religious zeal and revolted against Hellenism, had by now become increasingly steeped in the alien pagan culture. By the time of Jesus, their descendants, the Sadducees, had become an elite aristocratic class, devoid of spirituality and who sold their favors to the highest bidder.

[14] D.S.D. 8:12-14. It was under this same banner that John came baptizing from the wilderness.

[15] Some scholars dispute that this was not a Karaite but a rabbinical synagogue. In 809 CE an earlier cache of Dead Sea Scrolls had been found in

Among fragments of works which would later be discovered among the Dead Sea Scrolls, at the turn of the century, he found parts of a previously unknown text that would then be called the "Zadokite Fragment." Causing a major stir in the academic world, an extensive controversy over the age and historical importance of the text followed.

After the discovery of the Scrolls in 1947, it was recognized that these fragments were part of a copy of the Damascus Document found in several copies in the caves of Qumran. This was the Damascus Covenant, drawn up for those first embryonic Essenes in the wilderness of Damascus.[16]

From Damascus to wherever this Essenic movement spread, the call went out that the "Kingdom is at hand." All of the inter-testamental eschatological and apocalyptic pseudepigraphic books were scribed by Essene hands during these late Second Temple times.

Following in the general eschatological train of thought of the Book of Daniel,[17] which was also an important text for the Essenes, were written

---

caves in the same area as Qumran. Upon these scrolls, although not completely understood, the Karaites based their new offshoot sect from rabbinical Judaism. See J. Teicher, Journal of Jewish Studies, Vol II. No. 2., p.89f. Also, Hugh Schofield, The Essene Odyssey (1984), p. 47.

[16] It is interesting that Saul (Paul) was sent by the Sadducean High Priests to Damascus to arrest those of the Way. I would suggest that those of the Way(an Essene appellation) were not only believers but included other Essenes. It would be more plausible that he was sent after the Zadokites, the real enemy of the Temple priesthood. After his conversion, Paul was instructed and then spent three years in the "wilderness of Damascus" before going up and presenting himself to James and the apostles on Mount Zion. The three year period was the time needed for one to attend and graduate from the Essene Academy. Paul was a Pharisee. The Essenes followed an entirely different creed. They even had an additional sixth book of Torah. This is the Temple Scroll opened and deciphered by the famous Israeli scholar and archeologist Yigeal Yadin. Paul's letters are filled with euphemisms and parallels to sectarian verses and terms used in the Dead Sea Scrolls. Paul's emphasis upon the "mysteries," Sons of Light, and Sons of Darkness, etc., can only have been learned from the Essenes and not the Pharisees. His use of the term "Angel of Satan" corresponds with Essene doctrine, and especially the use of the term "Belial" (Hebrew: Blee-Ya'al meaning "utter worthlessness") as a proper name for Satan, connected with the "Light-Righteousness" and "Darkness - Lawlessness" in the same paragraph, and could have been read right out of the Qumran scrolls. This is the only place in the New Testament where the Essene "Belial" is used in place of "Satan." (2 Cor. 6:14-15) Jesus also uses the term "Sons of Light" when contradicting one of the adherents of the Way concerning contact with the unrighteous or "Sons of Darkness."

[17] Josephus informs us that by reason of the prophecy of the Book of Daniel, the Jews were expecting the coming of one who would rule the world. He also

13

such works as *Ben Sira, Enoch, The Testaments of the Twelve Patriarchs, Jubilees* and many other like works, many of which were found only among the Dead Sea Scrolls. The Essenic groups (of which there became many) waited upon the imminent war of the "Sons of Light" against the "Sons of Darkness" when the polluted Temple and its priesthood, as well as all the workers of evil, would be destroyed and the kingdom age would begin. The Kittim (Romans) and all of the idolaters would also meet their end in the wars of Gog and Magog. Then, a new Jerusalem and a pure Temple would come down from Heaven where a son of Zadok would again stand to the holy anointing and the Edenic age would begin.

We will interrupt the history of the Essene movement here in order to set forth the second infamous historical misdeed performed by the Hasmoneans upon their nation.

The Seat of David Usurped

Although the throne of David had remained unoccupied since the last anointed of the line had been exiled by Nebuchadnezzar to Babylon, the expectation had continuously remained that the righteous king of Israel would once again hold the scepter. With each national calamity, the anguished cry grew louder, yet the throne of Judah remained unoccupied. And then it happened!

Aristobulus the Hasmonean placed the crown upon his head and proclaimed himself the "King of the Jews,"[18] thereby, in one bold stroke, he officially usurped the throne of David. Thus, the Hasmonian house had usurped both messianic offices from their rightful heirs. Messianic zeal flared in both the ancient houses of Zadok and David and the revolt was on. These are the two messiahs imminently expected by the Essenes as recorded in the Dead Sea Scrolls. It was in these chaotic times that messiah came to be spelled with a capital "M."

David and Zadok

Although possibly already the High Priest under Saul, Zadok became the hereditary father of the High Priestly line by the appointment of

---

stated that Daniel was the only prophet who gave timetables to the end of the age.

[18] Josephus ANT. XIII, XI-1 Here, Josephus informs us that this was the first king since the Babylonian captivity, 481 years and 3 months earlier.

David. These two messianic (anointed) houses were, from the very first, intimately linked. It could be said that David and Zadok had anointed each other. When in David's last days, Adonijah plotted to usurp the throne, David instructed Zadok and Nathan the prophet to anoint Solomon king. For this loyal service Zadok was appointed High Priest. Upon his anointing by Zadok,[19] Solomon became the first anointed son of David, and is therefore considered the prototype of "Messiah, son of David." Thus was David's line established.

The Essene movement spread throughout regions in Syria, including Antioch. At some point, the mother group was joined by the elusive "Teacher of Righteousness," a Zadokite priest. This revered leader became among his followers the prototype of the priestly messiah which would bring in the Kingdom age spoken of by the Prophets. It seems that sometime in the last half of the second century BCE, this righteous teacher was hunted down and martyred by the "Wicked Priest"[20] of the Hasmonean house. Thereafter, the Essenes believed that their righteous teacher would return (possibly be resurrected) after forty years.[21]

In his new role as priest after the order of Melchizedek, he would act as final judge of the wicked. Leading the heavenly armies and the "Sons of Light" he would destroy the "Sons of Darkness" and vanquish *Belial* (Satan) and thus bring in the Kingdom.

The Essene movement spread widely in the final days of the second commonwealth. From the "wilderness of Damascus" across the Golan and down into the lower Galilee, including around the Sea of Galilee, new converts came mostly from among the *am-ha-aretz* (lower peasant classes).

Among the subgroups of this movement came the pre-Christian Nazarenes. These Essenes were evidently champions of the messiah of the Davidic line, judging from the names of some of their principal centers such as *Kochav* ("Star") on the southern Golan, and *Nazareth*[22] ("Shoot") in the Galilee. From among these peasants and fishermen, Jesus took his first disciples.

---

[19] See 1Kings:38-48
[20] Antichrist
[21] According to their calculation of the final date of Daniel's "seven weeks" prophecy.
[22] It is interesting that nowhere in the New Testament contemporary histories is there recorded a place name Nazareth. Not even the meticulous historian, Josephus, the commander of the Galilee during the Great Revolt, mentions the place. It is possible that the Davidic clan of Jesus had only recently settled this Galilee hilltop as a base for the rise of the imminently expected "shoot" from the stump of Jesse.

By the time of the destruction of the Jerusalem Temple, there were Essene groups spread throughout the land of Israel. Around the villages and cities, they established communities; they occupied the site of Khirbet Qumran, and, of course, kept a constant yet persecuted vigil in Jerusalem. Up against the Temple Mount on Mount Zion was the Essene quarter of the city with its own gate called the Essene Gate.

It should be noted here that by the first century CE, the Essene movement was made up of many subgroups: there were those who were celibate and those who took wives; there were those zealots who would take the kingdom by force; there were those who would take converts only after a three year period and under stringent rules of conduct and purity, while others, like John the Baptist and his disciples, and Jesus, would call all of the poor in spirit into the Kingdom. There were even inroads made into the Pharisee camp of those hoards who would be called to John's baptism. Ironically, even some Sadducees whom he chastised with fiery words,[23] came to John's baptism.

The Essene movement in those days might be compared to modern day Protestant denominations. Though their doctrines differed, sometimes dramatically, nearly all accepted the major Essene creed and saw the others as brothers.

The Stage is Set

"Now in those days John the Baptist came, preaching in the wilderness of Judea, and saying: 'Repent for the kingdom of heaven has drawn near' for this is He spoken of by Isaiah the prophet, saying: 'The voice of one crying in the wilderness, prepare the way of the Lord, make his paths straight ... But already the ax is even laid to the root of the trees...'" (Matt. 3:1-3, 10)

Dedicated to the Lord from birth as a Nazirite, it is written that "the child (John) grew and waxed strong in spirit and was in the deserts till the day of his showing unto Israel."(Luke 1:80)

I personally know the Judean desert well. It is a formidable place in both summer and winter. It is not the type of place that a child could hope to survive. But John was an Essene. He taught of the imminent

---

[23] If John called the Pharisees and Sadducees who came to him "offspring of vipers" and chased them away, then who were those masses whom he baptized? The only answer can be Essenes. Original Christianity is not in any way a Gentile phenomenon as popularly concluded, but arose within a strain of Judaism even more strict in their Jewish observances than the Pharisees.

Kingdom and performed the Essene baptism for the remission of sins.[24] John also taught that: "The one that has two tunics, let him give one to him that has not, and the one that has food, let him do the same." (Luke 3:11)

These are all strictly and exclusively Essene teachings as revealed in the Dead Sea Scrolls. Added to this, he was called the one "crying in the wilderness" of Isaiah 40:3. This was the very motto used by the Essenes to describe themselves. Josephus informs us that the Essenes adopted other peoples' children in order to raise them up in their way. I would suggest that the child, John,[25] given to the priests of Zadok by his mother,[26] was a resident member of the Essene Monastery (or caves) at Qumran until he began his ministry in exactly that area. He probably studied from the very scrolls now residing in the Shrine of the Book and Rockefeller Museum in Jerusalem.

Now Jesus came to John and was baptized of him. According to the Gospel of Luke he there was anointed with the Holy Spirit which fell upon him in the form of a dove.[27] Right after this, in Luke, Jesus' genealogy in the line of David is given. (Luke 3:21-31).

Now, after the baptism of John and a forty-day fast in the wilderness, Jesus (Yeshua Ben Yoseph Ben David) stepped into the pages of history proclaiming: "The time has been fulfilled and the kingdom of God draws near. Repent and believe the good news." (Mark 1:15)

In proclaiming the Gospel of the Kingdom, Jesus aligned himself with the Essenes. In calling for another kingdom like the Essenes, he proclaimed the illegitimacy of the current kingdom.[28]

In turning over the money changers' tables and predicting the destruction of the Temple, he proclaimed the illegitimacy of the magnificent Temple of Herod and its heretic priesthood, and in quoting the prophets, "I desire mercy and not sacrifice (Matt. 9:13) ... and the

---

[24] The Essenes held that repentance and baptism would stand for the abolition of sins in place of the profane sacrifices in the polluted Temple.

[25] John was himself a priest, as was Elijah. John's disciples continued his personal movement after his death. The Baptist movement in fact considered John to be the priestly messiah expected by the Essenes. These Mandeans yet exist in small number in southern Iraq. They call themselves Nazarenes.

[26] John was from the same priestly ancestral family as the Zadok clan.

[27] As Isaiah had written (Isa 11:2)

[28] By now, the Kingdom had digressed to the Herods under Roman tutelage. The Herods were of the stock of Edom, the ancient tribe of the South, force converted by the Maccabees. By the most ethnic of Hebrew families, they were not even considered to be Jewish, and by others, only half-Jews, definitely without credentials to sit upon the throne of Israel.

knowledge of God more than burnt offerings"(Hosea 6:6), he proclaimed along with the Essenes an alternative means of atonement.

Besides his obvious displeasure with the Temple and the sacrificial system, nowhere in the New Testament is it clearly recorded that Jesus ever offered sacrifices, an otherwise consistent practice for an observant or righteous Jew in the time when the Temple stood.[29] Even in his parable of the Good Samaritan, he denigrated the priests and Levites of his time (Luke 10:25-37).

In the end, Jesus, a peasant Galilean, stood up in front of Caiaphas, the Sadducean High Priest of his time, and confronted him to his face. To contradict the High Priest was considered a sacrilege. (John 18:19-24).

It should be noted here that among all of the differing parties (Sadducees, Pharisees, etc.) mentioned in the New Testament, the party of the Essenes is never mentioned. This omission becomes understandable when one considers that both Jesus' and John the Baptist's positions were aligned with those of the Essenes, and one does not regularly mention oneself in a third person context[30].

The Throne of David

There is an oddity recorded in the New Testament which, if one did not know the geographical and political layout of Jerusalem in the time of Jesus, would go unnoticed. The oddity concerns the location of the Last Supper.

In the heart of the Essene Quarter, straight from inside the Essene Gate, on the crest of Mount Zion, was the Tomb of David. Directly above this ancient chamber a ceremonial upper room had been constructed. This was assuredly a holy place for the Essenes where lay the remains of the first "anointed" one of the Lord from the stump of Jesse.

---

[29] Since the construction of the First Temple, Jewish sacrifices were allowed only here, performed only under the authority of the Temple priesthood. Sacrificial offerings to *YHWH* upon every hilltop altar, as in earlier times, was forbidden.

[30] The Essenes had many personal appellations of themselves. They were those of the Way, the *Yahad*, ("those who have become one") the Elect, the Poor, the New Covenanters, the Sons of Light, etc.

Although the ancient historians recorded conflicting practices among the different trends of the Essenes,[31] all agreed that all the trends followed a strict hierarchical code. Certainly, this code and its strict enforcement of the various levels of authority would have been in full sway in the Essene enclave on Mount Zion. Here, and in the entire Essene Quarter, the adherents of the faith awaited in earnest the imminent advent of the messiahs of Aaron and Israel. The Tomb of David would most assuredly be guarded and administered by the highest echelon: the priests of Zadok or their representatives. And yet, Jesus only had to send his disciples to the prearranged site: "and he said, 'go into the city to a certain one and say to him, "The Master says, my time is near. To you I will prepare the Passover with my disciples."'" (Matt 26:18)

With the chief priests and their henchmen after him in the city (Mark 14:1-2; Luke 22: 1-2), there had previously been arranged a signal of a man carrying a water jug: "and he will show you a large upper room which he has spread. Prepare there. And, going they found as He had told them, and they prepared the Passover."[32] (Luke 22:12-13)

This was not just some weary pilgrim coming up to the feast seeking accommodations, but a son of David whose hour had come, celebrating his prearranged Passover *seder* with His twelve disciples, literally, upon the throne of David.

It stands to reason that for the Zadokites who controlled the Essene Quarter and the holy site, and who had previously prepared the upper room, the long awaited Messiah from the House of David had come to His throne.

It was in this same place, according to the second chapter of the Book of Acts, that the promised comforter fell upon the disciples in tongues of fire, and in this same place James, the brother of Jesus, and the apostles, set up the first church on strict Essene guidelines (Acts 2:44-47, 4:32-35).

---

[31] This is also borne out in the conflicting doctrines and the contradictions between the various scrolls of the Essene Library from Qumran. The base library of scrolls, collected and guarded by the Essenes, was to become the source material from which to instruct those of the New Covenant when the imminently expected Kingdom arrived.

[32] Probably expected by Caiaphas and the Temple priests to come up to the Temple and raise a tumult on the eve of the feast, Jesus could reasonably expect to remain unmolested in this section of the city. Here he could in peace and safety, partake of the *seder* with his disciples. The Essene Quarter on the eve of Passover was no place for Sadducees. They could easily be recognized by their modern Hellenistic dress and manner.

19

It was here also that an edict was given under the authority of James and Peter that allowed uncircumcised Gentiles into the body of believers subject to the moral laws of Noah.[33]

James the Just was the first bishop of the Jerusalem Church. After he was murdered by the Sadducean High Priest,[34] Simeon, son of Cleophas of the line of David and cousin to Jesus and James, was instated in his stead. After this, a line of bishops from the family of Jesus became the official guardians of the throne of David.[35]

This familial succession to leadership of the early church would not have been possible at such an important site in the strictly structured Essene quarter unless these were themselves highly regarded Essenes. I believe that these Nazarenes[36] were the Essene champions of the long awaited Messiah from the House of David.

Modern Catholic scholars would refute that these Nazarenes actually sat upon the throne of David. In his article in *Biblical Archaeological Review* (May/June 1990) "Church of the Apostles Found on Mount Zion," Bargil Pixner, the Catholic archaeologist and historian from Mount Zion contends that the traditional tomb of David is not the genuine location. In the third paragraph of his article he states that " ... [it] is not really disputed by any serious body of scholarship. That is, that

---

[33] This was after a dispute in Antioch, twenty years after the crucifixion, between Paul and a delegation sent from James over the eligibility of uncircumcised converts. (Gal. 2:12-13) If this dispute came up only after 20 years, then until this time the church (synagogue) consisted exclusively of Jewish Nazarenes.

[34] In Hegesippus Memoirs, quoted by Eusebius, it is recorded that James was set upon the pinnacle of the Temple (the very pinnacle upon which Jesus was tempted of Satan) by the Sadducean High Priest, Joseph, and asked "Who is the door?" to which he answered "He sits on the right of the supreme power." At this he was thrown down from the Temple wall (Hegesippus Quoted by Eusebius) (Eccl. Hist. Bk 2, Chap., 23:12) For this evil, the High Priesthood was taken from Joseph, who was "very insolent" and "very rigid in judging offenders," by King Agrippa after a demonstration by the "most equitable of the citizens." In this rendition, Josephus claims that James was stoned (ANT XX, IX: 1) Another legend has it that James was thrown down the famous Temple steps and beaten to death with a weaver's beam.

[35] The tomb of David was certainly in need of a continuous guard. The Maccabean High-Priest and hero, John Hyrcanus, had, with no respect for David or his royal line, looted the sumptuous ancient tomb of its treasures to pay tribute to Antiochus the Pious in order to stop his siege on the city. It is here implied by Josephus that from this tomb of "the richest of all kings," Hyrcanus had money enough that "relying on this wealth, maintained foreign troops." (ANT. XIII, VIII: 4 WARS I,II :5). Later, King Herod would also attempt to rob the tomb.

[36] Translated from Hebrew as "shoots" or "sprouts" (from the stump of Jesse) *Notzri* is still used in modern Hebrew as the word for "Christian."

20

the structure in which the traditional tomb of David is located on Mount Zion is really a Roman period synagogue and not the tomb of David." He goes on to inform us that the original Mount Zion and the tombs of the Davidic royal line are probably to be found on the lower eastern hill of the City of David. Pixner does admit, though, "indeed that Zion has been something of a moveable mountain" as has David's tomb.

He also admits that through the muddling of time and destructions of the city, no one really knows anymore. He informs us that "the last person we know of who knew the exact location of David's tomb was Rabbi Akiva." The revered Rabbi of second Judean Revolt fame; Rabbi Akiva proclaimed Bar Kochba "King Messiah."

I concede that there is a possibility that David's tomb was originally on the lower hill, yet there is justifiable reason to think otherwise. For one, Josephus, who lived while the Temple and other Jerusalem monuments yet stood, and had an intimate knowledge of the layout of the city, placed Zion on the western traditional hill.[37] If Zion was originally to be found upon the eastern hill, then the first century occupants of the city did not know of this fact.

Yet, there is more compelling evidence to support the traditional contention that Zion and David's tomb were to be found upon the higher western hill. Even if the eastern hill was the original location, the first century Nazarenes believed it to be on the western and traditional site. In the second chapter of Acts, we find a straightforward statement that on the first Pentecost, the Paraclete descended in tongues of fire at our site, and it was in this place that Peter gave his famous Pentecost sermon. I believe that this sermon and the whole of Acts chapters one and two are, in part, a clear testimony that proclaims the existence and the purpose of the planting of the original Nazarene base on top of Mount Zion.

The witness, Luke, informs us that these were all of one tribe of men: i.e., Galileans (from the Nazarene enclave based upon Damascus and not Jerusalem). Acts 1:15 tells us that the original *Kahal* "assembly" numbered about 120 adherents. All of these were Galilean Nazarenes. It is obvious that this Essene sect was formed of those who followed the legacy of the House of David, "and all were amazed and marveled, saying to one another, Behold are not all these, those speaking, Galileans?" (Acts 2:7)

Peter opens his sermon by showing the words of the Holy Spirit being spoken by David (Acts 1:16) and then he quotes the psalms of David. In Acts 2:25-28 Peter introduces Jesus as the expected one quoted from the

---

[37] Josephus, WARS, Book 5: Chapter 4, (143) "Jerusalem"

21

mouth of David: "For David said as to Him, 'I always foresaw the Lord before Me, because He is at My right hand, that I not be moved. For this reason My heart rejoiced, and My tongue was glad; and My flesh also will dwell on hope, because You will not leave My soul in Hades, nor will You give Your Holy One to see corruption. You revealed to Me paths of life; You will fill Me with joy with Your face.'"

In Acts 2:29, Peter mentions David again; only this time, he speaks of the tomb of David: "Men, brothers, it is permitted to say to you with plainness as to the patriarch David, that he both died and was buried, and his tomb is among us until this day." This quote is from the *Interlinear Bible*, (Hendrickson Publishers). Other translations put David's tomb variously as either "with us" or "among us." The Greek word here translated is *en*. There are other common words, besides *en*, used in the Greek for both "with" and "among." *En* is better translated as "in, on, at, before and within."

In the Concordant Greek Text, which I believe to be the most literal English translation from the Greek, Peter says thus: "The memorial tomb of him is in us until the day this." Here it is obvious to me that Peter, after introducing Jesus the Nazarene "shoot" as the anointed Messiah from the mouth of David, can point to the tomb administered by the Nazarenes right there in that place.

Eusebius writes in his *Demenstratio Evangelica* that this place was no other than Zion: "This is the word of the gospel, which through our Lord Jesus Christ and through the Apostles went out from Sion and was spread to every nation. It is a fact that it pored forth from Jerusalem and Mount Sion adjacent to it, on which our Savior and Lord had stayed many times and where he had taught much doctrine."

I believe that it is well-documented that Zion indeed was known to be the western hill and that, even if not, our Nazarenes believed themselves to be occupying the true site. This whole argument, then, becomes demonstratively irrelevant to this study.

What is entirely mind-boggling to me is the fact that none of the modern historians or Scroll scholars have managed to unlock the meaning of the Dead Sea Scrolls. In missing the Zadok connection they simply miss the massive late Second Temple Zadokite explosion that it sparked, with all of its implications for later Judaism, Christianity and world culture. Zadok is simply written all over the Scrolls. Yet, for modern scholars the Sadducees are only Hellenized elites and not "Wicked Priest" usurpers of the profaned Temple as the Zadokites saw them.

In the book *James the Brother of Jesus*, by Robert Eisenman[38] (the most recent authoritative volume which I have read on this subject), the author refers us to a quote from Josephus:

"There was now enkindled mutual enmity and class warfare between the High Priests on the one hand and the priests and leaders of the masses of Jerusalem on the other. Each of the factions formed and collected for itself a band of the most reckless innovators, who acted as their leaders. And when they clashed, they used abusive language and pelted each other with stones. And there was not even one person to rebuke them."[39]

Rightfully attributing this instance to the tumult and rioting during the time when James the Just was martyred, Eisenman presumes these "priests" of the masses to have been "lower priests." I would suggest that these priests of the "masses" would rather be the higher Essene priests loyal to Zadok and the old-time religion, especially when we consider that the early Nazarene movement counted "a great crowd of the priests" among their recent converts. (Acts 6:7) Emanuel Testa calls these "priestly groups similar to those of Qumran."[40] It would stand to reason that for the Essenes who awaited both messiahs, a joining with those who awaited either one would be perfectly natural and, in fact, assured.

It is easy to understand why Eisenman and others might miss the point for two reasons. The first reason is that since the fall of the Temple, the role of Jewish priests has been drastically downgraded. The modern *Cohen* is a paper tiger with few responsibilities or privileges. Judaism has simply forgotten the all important role played by the priest in Torah Judaism. For the lack of the priestly role in the commandments of the Torah, all Jews are now considered ritually unclean.

When the priestly house of Zadok fell, so did the spiritual and physical trusteeship of the nation.

Onias III, the last of the line of legitimate High Priests, took his responsibilities as father of the nation as a sacred trust. Besides overseeing the purity of the sacrifices and Temple rituals, and the correct administration of the Law of God, Onias was also the nation's banker.

---

[38] Robert Eisenman, also co-author of *The Dead Sea Scrolls Uncovered*, and famous for co-authoring *the Facsimile Edition of the Dead Sea Scrolls*, is the Director of the Institute of Middle East Religions and Archeology, Judeo-Christian Origins at California State University, Long Beach.

[39] Josephus, Antiquities: 20.180 (Quoted by Eisenman, R., *James the Brother of Jesus*, page 318

[40] Testa, Emmanuel, *The Faith of the Mother Church*, p.13. See also Bargil Pixner "Jerusalem's Essene Gateway," *Biblical Archaeological Review*, May/June 1997 issue.

Like other contemporary temples to the deities, such as those of Baal and Ishtar, the Temple in Jerusalem contained the treasury of the nation. The Temple treasury was considered inviolable. The financial and, therefore, the political stability of Judea and the whole Jewish world depended upon this. If this sacred trust should be violated, and the treasury looted, then all vestiges of sovereignty and independence of the Jewish nation would be in jeopardy. If the Jewish economy should be undermined, then all that would remain would be vasselship and slavery to pagan foreign powers. This was the spiritual and political weight that fell upon the shoulders of one righteous man. Onias guarded the deposits of the Temple treasury with his life. In the end he lost both.

"But Heliodorus, because of the orders he had from the king (Epiphanius), said that this money must in any case be confiscated for the king's treasury. So he set a day and went to direct the inspection of these funds. There was no little distress throughout the whole city. The priests prostrated themselves before the altar in their priestly vestments and called toward heaven upon him who had given the law about deposits, that he should keep them safe for those who had deposited them. To see the appearance of the High Priest was to be wounded at the heart, for his face and the change in his color disclosed the anguish of his soul. For terror and bodily trembling had come over the man, which plainly showed to those who looked at him, the pain lodged in his heart. People also hurried out of their houses in crowds to make a general supplication because the holy place was about to be brought into dishonor. Women girded with sackcloth under their breasts, thronged the streets. Some of the young women who were kept indoors[41] ran together to the gates, and some to the walls, while others peered out of the windows. And holding up their hands to heaven, they all made supplication. There was something pitiable in the prostration of the whole populace and the anxiety of the High Priest in his great anguish." [42]

The second and main reason that scholars might miss the Zadok connection is that Josephus, our chief source for this period, I believe, purposefully buried Zadok by omission. It is well known among scholars that Josephus, although he praises his own truthfulness, yet gives biased renditions discoverable from other sources. And Josephus had much reason to be biased. He wrote under the lustrous conditions of empirical sanction and sanctuary. A turncoat Jewish general of the

---

[41] The virgin daughters of Zion
[42] 2Maccabees 3:13-21

24

Galilee[43] during the revolt, he rode in with Titus and watched the Temple burn. Politically, Josephus was forced to turn toward Rome with his back toward those heroes of the revolt. He was afterward hated by his countrymen.

Josephus would bring those Zealot heroes of Masada, who finished their lives, man, woman and child, down to the nasty little daggermen-stabbers running amok in the Temple courtyards. He simply could not stand on the side of those fellow countrymen and patriots who so stiff-neckedly and violently opposed his patron, Rome. The Zealots were among the leaders of the opposition to the Sadducean priesthood.[44] Josephus documents them with disgust, yet he had an even weightier reason to bury Zadok.

Josephus was a priest and prince of the Hasmonean royal court. He was politically family related, through his mother, to the Maccabean usurpers of the High Priesthood. Although he praises the virtues of the Essenes, he never lets you know about their principal concerns. To Josephus, Zadok was opposite and opposing to his own royal house. His own claim to royalty and exalted status before Rome,[45] in fact, depended upon Zadok's dismissal.

Josephus, who recorded even trivial, meticulous details[46] in his exhaustive works, could never have missed the important and legendary reign of the House of Zadok. Zadok, the ancestor, had carried the Ark of the Covenant through the countryside with David in the latter's travails. He had also carried the Ark into its permanent resting place, beyond the veil in the First Temple of Solomon. His family reigned with few interruptions through both Temple periods up until Antiochus IV Epiphanius and the denouncement of Onias III.

Josephus has much praise for the Maccabees, yet passes over Zadok with a silent whisper. When informing us of the fall of the Zadokite dynasty, he passively states, " ... and driving away the son of Onias the Third, put Jacimus into the High Priest's place, one that was indeed of the stock of Aaron, but not of the family of Onias.[47] No clue here.

When speaking of the rival temple in Leontopolis Egypt, Josephus informs us that Onias asked permission of Ptolemy and Cleopatra "that

---

[43] Josephus held command over Essene territory.
[44] Even the Pharisees had demanded that the Hasmoneans must step down from the High Priesthood
[45] The ruling Sadducean High Priesthood stood loyal to Rome until the bitter end.
[46] Even to the point of recording the biting off of the ears of a contender to the High Priesthood, therefore rendering him blemished and unfit for office.
[47] Josephus, Antiquities, XX, X

25

he might build a temple in Egypt like that at Jerusalem, and might ordain Levites and priests out of their own stock." [48]

These statements prove that it is possible to tell the truth and hold it back at the same time. Still no clue to the important hierarchy of Zadok or to the usurpation. Josephus would have us believe that the transition from the house of Zadok to his own Maccabean line went normally and peacefully. The Scrolls tell another story. [49]

The Essenes thereafter awaited only the Messiah of Aaron: the "teacher of righteousness" and son of Zadok. Under the banner of Melchizedek, this priestly messiah would lead the heavenly armies and join the battle of the "Sons of Light" against the "Sons of Darkness" of the War Scroll. The returned Messiah of David would also take part in this scenario.

In this forthcoming battle, Belial (Satan) and his demonic armies, the Kittim (Romans) and all the Sons of Darkness would be defeated. The polluted Temple would be destroyed and a new Jerusalem with a new pure Temple would come down from heaven. The Messiahs of Aaron and David would then take their rightful chairs and the Kingdom age would begin.

But this was not to be. In 70 CE, Titus and his Roman legions swept down on Jerusalem and destroyed the magnificent Temple of Herod. When the conflagration had ended and the rivers of blood dried black on the marble paving stones, not one stone was left upon another of what had been the Temple of YHWH. [50]

Qumran had been destroyed a few years earlier, with its treasured library of scrolls undiscovered and hidden for nearly two thousand years. Evidently, there remained alive not one of the residents of Qumran who knew the whereabouts of the hidden scrolls. Some Qumranites probably fled to the nearby mountain fortress of Massada and met their end there in 73 CE along with the Zealots, [51] themselves a militarily active subgroup of the Essenes. [52]

---

[48] Josephus, Antiquities, XIII, III, 1
[49] Josephus, like us, could not have known of the hidden Qumran scrolls.
[50] Legend has it that the plunderers of the Temple pried loose the remaining foundation stones in order to recover the gold and precious metals turned to glowing liquid by the conflagration, which found the lowest points of gravity between the seams.
[51] The Zealots continued the revolt among the large Jewish community in Egypt. Initially meeting with success, the revolt was eventually quashed by Rome.
[52] Fragments of Qumranite sectarian scrolls were found among the ruins by Yaegal Yadin.

The Messiah of Aaron had not come. The forces of darkness had prevailed in a then time Armageddon. There was no New Jerusalem and no Kingdom. Only drawn faces, torn sack cloth, and dust remained.

The Nazarenes, following Jesus' instructions had fled Zion to the hills of Judea (actually Pella in Transjordan), but they soon returned to their custodianship of the upper room of the Tomb of David. There a hierarchy of heredity from the family of Jesus guarded the Throne of David until 135 CE. In that year, Bar Kochba was defeated and Hadrian converted the city of Jerusalem into the pagan *Aelia Capitolina*, forbidding Jews from residing in the city.[53]

So, what of the messiah of Aaron? The Nazarenes continued to occupy the Canacle on Zion for 65 years after the fall of the Temple. Why had their hopes not been dashed when the priestly messiah had failed to appear? Why did they not break up in defeat and go home as the disciples had after the crucifixion?

The Essenes understood from what had been written of the Kingdom age by the prophet Zechariah there were to be two messiahs, [54]"and I answered and said to him, what are these two olive trees? ... What are the two clusters of olives which are beside the two golden pipes, emptying the golden oil from themselves? ... and he said, these are the two sons of fresh oil who stand by the Lord of the whole earth." (Zech 4:11, 12, 14)

Although the *Manual of Discipline* speaks of the "the coming of a prophet and the anointed ones (*meshiche*: plural) of Aaron and Israel,[55] the Damascus Document, on the other hand, hints that these two might come as one: "The Messiah (singular) of Aaron and Israel."[56]

As previously mentioned, the Essenes had cast their martyred "Teacher of Righteousness" in a new role on his expected return: the priesthood of Melchizedek[57] Thus he would return in a new, heavenly, priestly line.

[And it will be proclaimed at] the end of days concerning the captives as [He said ... *to proclaim liberty to the captives* ... (Isa. 61:1)[58] Its interpretation is that He] will assign them to the Sons of Heaven and to the inheritance of Melchizedek,[or He will cast] their [lot] amid the portions of Melchizedeck, who will return them there and will proclaim to

---

[53] Even after 135 CE, the Nazarenes made secret pilgrimages to the site, and in fact reestablished a weak presence there.
[54] This is borne out in many of the Essene books such as the Testaments of the Twelve Patriarchs, etc.
[55] 1 QS IX:10, 11
[56] C.D. XII: 23; XIV:19; XIX:10
[57] Hebrew: "King of Righteousness"
[58] This is the passage in which Jesus referred to himself: "*The* Spirit of *the* Lord is upon Me ... "

them liberty, forgiving them [the wrong-doings] of all their iniquities. And this thing will [occur] in the first week of the Jubilee that follows the nine Jubilees. And the Day of Atonement is the end of the tenth Jubilee, when all the Sons of Light and the men of the lot of Melchizedek will be atoned for [and] a statute concerns them with their rewards. For this is the moment of the year of grace for Melchizedik.[59]

Again, in Zechariah we read that the Man whose name is The Branch who will build the Temple of the Lord, shall sit as a priest and king upon his throne. (Zech 6:12-13). Jesus cast himself in the priesthood of Melchizedek when he proclaimed before Caiaphas the Sadducean High Priest: "I tell you more. From this time you shall see the Son of man sitting off *the* right *hand* of power, and coming on the clouds of the heavens.[60] Then the High Priest tore his garments ..." (Matt. 26:64-65)[61]

For the Essenes,[62] he who would be "coming in the clouds of the heavens" was no other than Melchizedek. Thus it is seen that for the early Jewish believers, Jesus, in the priesthood of Melcheizedek overrode Caiaphas and the Aaronic line. Although He arose from Judah, yet he became both King and Priest (Heb. 6:13-20)[63]

Nearly two thousand years later, Tech Oteeoos, an aged Greek monk, went to digging on Mount Zion in the forbidden ground in what then was "no mans' land" between Israel and Jordan. What he found, we now with a sense of awe, history and humility, present to you and the world: *The Messianic Seal of the Jerusalem Church.*

---

[59] Vermes, G., *The Dead Sea Scrolls in English*, p. 301
[60] Jesus here seems to have referred to a quote from the Essene book of Enoch, as also did his brother Jude. (Jude 14-15)
[61] In light of the arguments presented in this essay, yet another New Testament mystery is cleared up, that is: Why did the High Priests concern themselves so strongly in having Jesus crucified? It would otherwise be below the dignified status of the High Priest to trump up charges to force the gruesome murder of a simple Galilean and fellow Jew at the hands of pagan foreigners.
[62] Besides the early Christians, Essene sects continued to exist after the fall of the Temple, such as the Mandeans (the followers of John the Baptist), the Hemerobaptists, the Therapeutae, the Bana'im, the Maghariya and Gnostic sects such as those who collected the Judeo-Christian Nag Hamadi manuscripts.
[63] This is not the first instance whereby a son of David became a priest. In 2Samuel 8:17-18 both Zadok and David's sons were named priests: "...and the sons of David were priests."

28

CERTIFICATE OF AUTHENTICITY

This is to certify that on February 11, 1999, Rueven Schmalz, a sculptor, residing in Livnim, Israel under the supervision and in the presence of Raymond R. Fischer, MACM, President of Olim Creative Products, Ltd., of Tiberias, Israel took direct "strikes" from two ancient Christian artifacts.

These artifacts are certified by their owner, Herr Ludwig Schneider of Jerusalem, Israel to be two of eight such ancient relics that he personally received in 1990 from a Greek/Orthodox monk who had excavated them from a site on Mount Zion in the 1960's. Herr Schneider certifies herewith that one of these pieces, containing the copyrighted symbol: "Seven branched Candelabra/Star of David/Fish," also known as "The Messianic Seal of the Jerusalem Church," with a small and unique cross symbol in the body of the fish portion of the symbol, and the ancient Aramaic lettering that is translated as: "For the Oil of the Spirit" has been validated by a Professor of Archeology from the University of Dortmund, Germany, and by an Israeli Professor of Archeology as having originated in the late first to early second centuries. The authenticity of the artifacts is further established by an earlier discovery by Bedouins in the Judean Desert south of Jerusalem in 1963, of a small silver artifact (*lamina*) which was found with the exact same inscription as on the "stand" artifact: "For the oil of the Spirit." The form of the Aramaic letters on the two pieces are so intrinsically exact, as to have possibly been scribed by the same hand. This tiny piece (6cm x 2cm) has been separately dated to the first century.

The undersigned believe that it is highly probable that the rectangular stone "stand" artifact piece was used as a stand upon which was placed a vial of anointing oil in the Early Christian Church on Mount Zion, founded and first pastored by James the Just, the brother of Jesus. All eight relics handed over personally to Herr Schneider were found in close proximity to this ancient church site.

The second "strike" was taken by the sculptor from the face of an ancient clay pottery vial. There is a prominent rendition of the "Messianic Seal of the Jerusalem Church" etched on the face of the vial. While there can be no certainty regarding the purpose of this vessel, the undersigned speculate that it may well have been used as a container and dispenser of anointing oil.

By our signatures below, we attest that to the best of our knowledge and belief all of the above information is entirely true.

Ludwig Schneider
Editor-in-chief
News About Israel
Jerusalem, Israel

Reuven Schmalz
Sculptor
Livnim, Israel

Raymond R. Fischer, MACM
President
Olim Creative Products, Ltd
Tiberias, Israel

A Eight early Second Century Christian artifacts displaying the Messianic Seal of the Jerusalem Church. All were found in the ancient grotto near the Tomb of David on Mount Zion in the 1960's by Tech Oteeoos who presented them to Ludwig Schneider in 1990.

B. "Anointing Oil Vial" artifact standing on top of the "anointing oil stand" artifact displaying the ancient Hebrew lettering meaning "For the oil of the Spirit." It is likely, we believe, that these pieces were used by the twelve apostles during initiating ceremonies of new believers in the sacred grotto of the Jerusalem Church.

C. An Ancient pottery shard artifact with painted Messianic Seals and clearly rendere[d] "shoots" as a border design.

D. Ancient Roman Lamp bearing Messianic Seal of the Jerusalem Church. It was we believe, likely used to illuminate the ancient grotto during the Baptism of Fi[re] administered to new believers who were coming into the Jerusalem Church shor[tly] after the ascension of Jesus.

E. An ancient pottery shard showing an interesting variation of the Messianic Sea[l.] We believe that the heavy dots that make up the menorah could have also bee[n] a representation of a fruiting fig tree.

An Explanation of the Symbol

The Messianic Seal of the Jerusalem Church, copyrighted as "Seven Branched Candelabra/Star of David/Fish," is unlike any of the early Judeo Christian graffito. Besides the use of the *Taw*[64] or cross sign as the fish's eye on the "anointing stone" artifact, this seal stands apart. It is also the most Jewish of all the other Nazarene graffiti and seals.[65]

No early Christian Gentile group would have ever used this seal. The Gentile church of those early ages were trying to distance themselves from the Jews as a political necessity.[66] The period of its use on Mount Zion could only have been from the crucifixion in 30 to 135 CE, just over a century, making the "Seal" exclusively Jewish and Nazarene.

The "Seal," consisting of three parts in a vertical line, in light of the findings and their implications suggested in this present writing, is deeply significant. To my mind, this "Seal" signifies the body of believers (the fish) connected through the stump of Jesse (Star) to the Holy of Holies (Candelabra) and therefore to God. It could also, therefore, signify the church's redemption through both messianic offices; i.e., the anointed of David and Aaron.

Yet, if one looks closely, there are actually only two images here. The third image, made up of the roots of the candelabra and fish, exists only in essence. The fish tends toward the earth, the worldly home of man, while the candelabra tends toward heaven, infinity and God. The essence of the Star of David, signifying the Stump of Jesse, thus becomes the unifying factor between God and man.

The significance of the seven-branched candelabra, we all know as standing before the holy of holies in the Temple of *YHWH*.

The Star of David is another case. Although it has been used since the Bronze Age, as presumably a magical sign, the first use on a Jewish

---

[64] The *Taw* is the final letter of the Hebrew alphabet which, in the archaic Proto Hebrew script used in the First Temple period,was in the form of a cross and was a pre-Christian sign. Possibly used by the Essenes, it was a "saving" sign. It was a sign to be marked upon the foreheads of the righteous in Ezekiel's prophetic vision, before the wicked of Jerusalem were to be destroyed, man, woman and child. (Ezek. 9:1-7)

[65] Other graffito inscribed in Judeo-Christian tombs, baptismals and sacred grottoes include the "cosmic ladder," (or sign of the seven heavens), the monogrammed cross.

[66] After the bloody revolt against Rome, anything Jewish or Judaic was considered anathema to the Empire. The Fathers realized that they could not hope to feed Rome a Judaized Christianity.

seal was from the seventh century BCE.[67] It was connected with Judeo-Christians in the extra-biblical "Testament of Solomon." It is not clear when the hexagram was first engraved on the seal or ring of Solomon, as recorded in the Talmud (GIT.68).

This star was also used as a sign of significance before the name of the deceased on a sixth century CE Jewish tombstone from Torento in southern Italy. It was also used as a graffito in early Judeo-Christian tombs, sometimes with a *Taw* in the center.

Though clouded in time, no one seems to know when the hexagram star was first attributed to David. I believe that we have found the first historical use of this star as attributed to David in the hands of the first Jewish church on the throne of David on Mount Zion. Presumably, later usage of the Star of David had its roots in this ancient predestruction memory from David's tomb on Mount Zion

The fish has been used from the earliest Christian times as a symbol of the church. Traditionally, the fish has also been symbolically associated with water baptism. The Essenes, as well as the Nazarenes were baptizers.

There is a hole, grated over with a steel mesh cage and iron bars near the apex of Mount Zion. In my younger days, I "ran" Mount Zion and the Walled City. Many times in the quiet shade of a summer afternoon I stood before this gap in the earth and tried to peer inside. The legends were that some great secrets were buried there. Some of those—my friends said they had heard that one of the Dead Sea Scrolls pinpoints this place as a hidden cache of Second Temple treasures;[68]and the most prevalent legend was that therein lay the long lost "Ark of the Covenant."

Little did I know then, that therein lay an almost equally precious treasure—the sacred grotto of the first Nazarene church. This area, dotted with *mikvahs* (baptismal pits) is situated in the immediate vicinity of the tomb of David. This was the dynamic heart of the Essene Quarter in Second Temple times. Now, it is a grassy deserted area shaded by tall and lonely Jerusalem pines.

Yet, in this pit, in pre-1967 no-man's-land, were found many pieces of first and second century pottery shards, oil lamps and stone pieces, all inscribed or embossed with the Messianic Seal of the Jerusalem Church. Among these various artifacts, for example, was found a brick shaped piece of local marble scribed with the Messianic Seal and the words in

---

[67] Found in Sidon, it belonged to Joshua B. Asayahu: Encyclopedia Judaica, s.v. "Magen David."
[68] This was the first time I had heard about the lone copper scroll found in one of the caves at Qumran.

ancient Dead Sea Scrolls era Aramaic "For the Oil of the Spirit." This seems to have been the base stand for a vial of anointing oil[69] Interestingly, a nearly intact small pottery flask with an inscribed Messianic Seal was found nearby. When I first considered the implications of the discovery, I immediately remembered that the first Pentecost,[70] as recorded in the New Testament where the Spirit[71] fell upon all in tongues of fire, had occurred in this very place on Mount Zion.

(of the Spirit)   (for the Oil)

This place was definitely a religious center and the insignia obviously more than ornamental graffito, judging by the large number of Messianic Seal bearing artifacts found in the same pit, and accompanied by baptismal fonts, at least one of which was marked with a Messianic Seal. This all at the throne of David and Nazarene base in the Essene Quarter on Mount Zion.

The early Judeo-Christians worshiped in sacred grottoes[72] (caves, or hewn chambers) as is evident from the large number of them excavated throughout Israel and wherever else their centers have been found. Whether used for mystery religious sites or for protection from their antagonizers, these chambers were artificially lit and often contained baptismals. Many times a staircase of seven steps, signifying the cosmic

---

[69] It is interesting to point out that James the Just, the leader of this first church, instructs his readers in the practice of anointing with oil for healing. (James 5:14)
[70] The Essenes of the Dead Sea Scrolls inducted new converts into the fold of those awaiting the New Covenant only once each year, on the day of Pentecost.
[71] The receiving of the Spirit as a consequence of anointing was known from the anointing of David himself: "And the LORD said, 'Arise anoint him: for this is he.' Then Shemu'el took the horn of oil, and anointed him in the midst of his brothers; and the spirit of the LORD came upon David from that day onwards." (1 Samuel 16:12-13 *The Jerusalem Bible*)
[72] Eusebius called them: "sacred and mystic caves." *De laudibus Constantini* IX (Pg 20, 1369)

ladder, led down into these underground grottos. Religiously significant graffito were normally etched into the walls.

Unquestionably used as places of worship, one can easily speculate that these grottos provided quiet and hidden away places for teaching, the reading of scripture, prayer, singing of psalms and other congregational activities. The artificial light illuminating the darkness signified the light of God and the Messiah

Judging from the ritualistic Messianic Seal artifacts found, including Roman period oil lamps, it is very likely that our still largely unexcavated pit is the grotto of the first Nazarene Church on Mount Zion.

Fortunately, in an earlier discovery by Bedouins in the Judean Desert south of Jerusalem in 1963, a small silver artifact (*lamina*) was found with the exact same inscription as on our oil stone: "For the oil of the Spirit." The form of the Aramaic letters on the two pieces are so intrinsically exact, as to have possibly been scribed by the same hand. This tiny piece (6cm x 2cm), found with Herodian oil lamps, is dated to the first century.

This *lamina* contains sixteen lines, most of which are Aramaic text. These describe for us what *our* oil stone means. In short, the decipherment is almost a carbon copy of James 5:14-16.

Testa, who deciphered this text, immediately connected it with the practice of anointing as set forth in the epistle of James.

This *lamina*, like others found in Syria and Lebanon (Essene territory) is a sort of *laisser-passer* (pass card) placed in the mouth of the deceased confirming his confession of faith, and proclaiming his salvation. Before being allowed the anointing with the holy oil which symbolized conversion, the Nazarene recipient must first have confessed his sins.

I believe that this *lamina* was issued to the recipient upon his conversion at the Nazarene base on Mount Zion. The Book of Acts records many conversions at this site under the administration of James the Just and the Apostles.

The one striking difference between the *lamina* and the text of James is that the former also reveals that the forgiveness of sins is accomplished without (Temple) sacrifice. This, to my mind, fits nicely with both Zadokite and specifically Nazarene doctrine opposing the Temple sacrifice.

Testa, after deciphering this *lamina* and having trouble with a few words, offered other scholars to come to his aid. J.T. Milik (of Dead Sea Scroll team fame) immediately took up this challenge. Although other scholars agreed with Testa, Milik tore the text apart. Forging some letters, and disregarding others he proclaimed Testa's decipherment faulty and proclaimed the piece unimportant, and he assigned it a date in the fifth or sixth century. This is the same Catholic priest and scroll scholar who sat on the lion's share of controversial "sectarian" fragments for over 40 years. Milik held these scroll fragments (along with De Vaux) close to his bosom and would reveal them to no one, especially not to Israeli Jews. As pointed out in *The Dead Sea Scrolls Deception*, these priests were emissaries of the Vatican.

James the Just and the apostles established on Mount Zion a Qumran-like Essene commune. As revealed in Acts, there was strict discipline and a hierarchy. It stands to reason that this group, with James at their head, would have immediately established Nazarene ritual, including a ceremonial healing and baptismal center which was to be the place where the mass conversions spoken about in Acts were sealed by anointing with oil and water immersion.

Our anointing stone had already been well worn, with the edges eroded from use when excavated. One large chip on the upper right corner of its face is prominent. Even the sharp edges of this chip have been eroded.

This is a hard piece of local marble. Only constant use over a considerable period of time could have caused this polishing of the once sharp edges. In my opinion, this piece came into use in the earliest Nazarene times at this site. Considering that James and the Apostles set up the baptismal center, maybe even before Pentecost, I believe that he and they administered "Oil of the Spirit" from this very stone base. That would make this piece, if my suspicions are correct, the earliest known (and the earliest possible) Christian artifact.

The obvious question now is, Why has this center and the Messianic Seal[73] been lost and forgotten for nearly two thousand years? And the second question, not less important, Why was the history of the true first church not duly recorded?[74]

Let us ask the Nazarenes' principal antagonist: the Holy Roman Catholic Church. I hold great respect for the Roman Catholic Church. The Catholic Church is certainly forthcoming and honest in clearly stating both its various positions and history. The Roman Catholic Church with confidence proclaims itself to be the "New Israel." With the God given right to change laws and customs, the church holds the "keys" by divine right, thus they call themselves catholic (genuine).

---

[73] Key to the Dead Sea Scrolls
[74] Except for Paul, there are no extended histories of the acts or letters of the Apostles. These, it must be remembered were the twelve supreme ambassadors appointed by Jesus to carry the word of the gospel to the world.

34

If it had not been for the Gentile church fathers, we would know nearly nothing about the Nazarene Church of the Circumcision. The Fathers, in their extensive polemical writings against these Judaizing "heretics," recorded much of their history and quoted from many of their now long lost books.

Since the first of the Dead Sea Scrolls was translated and studied in church hands, we have seen a flurry of Catholic historians vying to be the first to reopen this long lost chapter within their own good light.

I do not suggest that certain facts may not be suppressed by the church until they may be digested with a sweet stomach. The Messianic Seal is a case in point. The church has known about this discovery, perhaps even before it first broke from the earth to the light of day in the hands of a monk. Notwithstanding that, there may be a considerable cache of artifacts with this emblem in the cellars of the Israel Museum. Ironically, these are the very two antagonists (the Jewish authorities and the church) responsible for the demise of the Nazarene movement in the first place.

In 1990, Ludwig Schneider, a long time citizen of Jerusalem, visited an old Greek monk in his hovel dwelling. Ludwig's purpose was to get a look at some old artifacts bearing a unique seal which were in possession of the monk. He was shocked at what he saw. Immediately, Ludwig recognized these artifacts as Judeo-Christian, probably even from the first Nazarene church. Being a historian and scholar himself, he remembered that James the Just, the brother of Jesus, together with the other apostles had established their seat here.

Being led by the old monk to an iron grated pit near the tomb of David, he crawled over the much less imposing fence of that time and down inside. To his right, inside the pit, he found the Messianic Seal engraved on the stone wall. Rushing back to the priests of the Monastery to report his incredible find, he was shocked by the audience he received. Rebuffing him, they refused to answer his questions about the "Seal" and locked him outside of the Monastery gate.

Taking with him pictures he had taken of the eight seal embossed artifacts which he later received from the old monk as a gift, he next approached the Israel Museum of Jerusalem. He was told by the curator that the museum already had other pieces bearing the seal. Ludwig was then assured that there would be made a display of these artifacts in the museum and that the story would be told to the world.

When this had not transpired as promised, after the passing of years, in 1996 Ludwig opened a gift shop alongside many others selling Christian souvenirs in the Jewish Quarter of the Old City of Jerusalem.

This went fine until he began to sell souvenirs sporting the Messianic Seal. The Seal-embossed items sold well, and soon the neighboring gift shops, some run by orthodox Jews, began to copy and sell the Seal-embossed items.

In short order, Ludwig's shop was attacked and stoned by Haredi Jews. He was warned to remove this offending and "profane" emblem from his shelves. Immediately, the emblem disappeared from the shelves of the neighboring shops. The stoning attacks by the orthodox continued, and finally, after less than a year of operations, Ludwig closed his shop in 1997.

Whether or not this seal is being suppressed, it should be known to all that historical facts cannot be indefinitely hidden. Sooner or later, truth, like that of the Messianic Seal, makes its way into the light. It will be most interesting to see how Jewish Orthodoxy will deal with these (old) new historical implications. After all, it was the Jews of the time who gave James the title "Just" by reason of his great piety. How was it that, for 40 years, from the crucifixion to the fall of the Temple, the Nazarenes were allowed to administer the sacred tomb of David?

Could it be that originally the Pharisees and other Judeans accepted or even honored these Nazarene descendants of King David? It is an historical fact that in the broadly sectarian Judaism of that time the Nazarenes were not considered *minim* (heretics) until they refused to fight with their countrymen in the great revolt against Rome and the Bar Kocha revolt.

It must be stated here that there were those classes of Nazarenes who did not accept the decree of James at the Apostolic Council which accepted non circumcised Gentiles into the fold of believers. These Nazarene sub-groups such as the Ebionites therefore opposed the apostleship of Paul and counted him as a heretic.

The Gentile church fathers made good use of this fact in also condemning the original Jerusalem Nazarene church. To the church fathers, all of the original Jewish followers of Jesus were Judaizing heretics to be stamped out and their books banned. These Nazarene disciples of Jesus, following in the footsteps of their master, [75] held the ancient moral code of Moses in high esteem.[76]

In the pagan world of the first centuries of the first millennium there was no such supreme law code for the ordering of human society as was

---

[75] "The scribes and the Pharisees sat down on Moses' seat. Then all things, whatever they tell you to keep, keep and do ... " (Matt. 23:2-3)
[76] Acts 21:20

the Law of Moses. The ancient pagan rites generally led to the denigration of the majesty of those created in the image of God.[77]

Even Paul, the champion of grace, proclaimed that the definition of sin can only be judged by the Law,[78] and that the Law is holy, just and good.[79]

It is not by coincidence that the judicial systems of the western democratic societies are founded upon the Law of Moses. Many a small town American courthouse displays a table of the Ten Commandments before the broad front steps as a sign of justice.

From the outset, the church fathers condemned the Jewish Nazarenes in their polemical treatise against Judaizing heretics. Epiphanies, in his polemical work, *Panarion,* shows this general trend: "They were so called followers of the Apostles and for such people make a fine object to be refuted and are easy to catch, for they are Jews and nothing else."[80]

Eusebius[81] the Gentile bishop of Caesarea in his early church history[82] tells us much about the second century schism directed against the

---

[77] By the time Paul and Christianity had reached the Empire, paganism had begun to crumble. (Mithraism , Sun god Worship, imported to Rome by the Roman Legions had taken up some of the vacuum.) For this reason there were many God fearing Greeks gathered around the Diaspora synagogues among which Paul proselytized. These masses of disenchanted Gentiles were drawn to the morality and societal justice embodied within the Mosaic Law Code. The Roman Church, when it had taken control, reversed this Gentile-leaning toward Judaism, actually banning Gentile-Jewish intimate contact under punishment of death and banning Gentile conversion to Judaism. The church saw Judaism as a dangerous rival. Drawn into the vast vacuum of disintegrating paganism without the moral guidance of the Law of God, the church quickly took on the flavor and customs of the old pagan gods and rites. The institution of the "Day of the Sun," for instance was taken from Mithraism. Constantine had earlier converted to this sun deity before he adopted Christianity. His coins and banners yet carried Mithra's seals (the Unconquerable Sun) long after he converted to Christianity. The Vatican itself had formerly been an edifice devoted to Mithra. A fourth century Mitraem, from the time when Eusebius was Bishop there, has also recently been found in Caesarea.

[78] Romans 7:7

[79] Romans 7:12

[80] Panarion 29-5:4, 9:1

[81] Eusebius, on instructions from his friend, the Roman Emperor Constantine, personally engineered a de-Judaized Christianity acceptable to Rome. Constantine thus ordered it to be the official religion in 313 CE. Eusebius, a thorough historian also had access to many of the now lost Jewish Nazarene books for his reference in this endeavor. At first, mighty Rome fed Christians to the lions and they were forced into the catacombs. Yet, like a wildfire out of control, Christianity increasingly dominated over the feeble and fading pagan classes. Constantine was at an impasse. The Empire was at the brink of civil

Judeo Christians on the subject of Easter. The Nazarenes had always celebrated the Lord's Supper on the 14th of NISAN, or the Passover eve. Even many of the original eastern Gentile churches followed this custom. Pope Victor (189-199) instructed that church synods should meet on this subject in Caesarea, the Church See of Palestine. Only Gentile bishops attended, although there were many Judeo Christian groups in the Land.

Bellarmino Bagatti, the Franciscan archeologist and historian of Jerusalem, in his book *The Church from the Circumcision*[83] suggests that the Jewish bishops of the Land were intentionally boycotted from the meeting by the Gentile Bishops, so that the latter could decide for themselves on the Easter usage without opposition. As he writes: "The fixing of Easter on a Sunday resulted in a certain manner in taking from the hands of the Judeo-Christians a predominance ..." [84]

After this, a series of church councils beginning with Nicea, where the Easter Sunday usage was established, were called purposefully to marginalize the Nazarenes.[85] After Nicea, the fathers reunited in Antioch in 341 CE[86] to excommunicate anyone who would nullify the decree of Nicea concerning Easter.

Pixner, in his article, "Church of the Apostles Found on Mount Zion,"[87] provides insight into the interface of Nazarene and Gentile Christian worship and practices:

"Their adherence to Jewish customs, especially circumcision and observance of Jewish Holy days, naturally alienated them (the Nazarenes) from the church of the gentiles. The fissure became a gaping canyon with the strong anti-Judaic positions taken by the Byzantine church after the Council of Nicea (325 A.D.)

---

war and chaos, with the rebels set to win. With a genius mind, at the crossroads in history, Constantine made the right choice and the Empire flourished.

[82] HE 5, 23, 5

[83] page 81

[84] The Roman Church was making a strong effort to de-Judaize Christianity, in this case, by stopping the practice of the revered Jewish church partaking of the Lord's Supper on Passover evening as a keynote feature of the sacred Easter Weekend celebrations.

[85] The very point of Judeo-Christianity hinged upon the Paschal Lamb implications of Passover Eve. Only if the "blood was upon the doorposts" could one be "passed over" in the coming Armageddon before the Kingdom age.

[86] Canon I (Page 137, 1275-6)

[87] Pixner, Bargil. 1990. Church of the Apostiles Found on Mount Zon. *Biblical Archeological Review*, May/June, 17-18.

"Though recognizing the authenticity of the place, the gentile Christians looked with suspicion and almost contempt at the synagogue of Judeao-Christians on Mount Zion, considering their way of life outdated, if not heretical[88]

"This dispute, especially as it relates to Mount Zion, is referred to in a letter from church father Gregory of Nyssa, who visited Jerusalem in 381 A.D. Gregory reported that the very place that was the very first to receive the Holy Spirit was now in turmoil, and that a counter-altar had been set up. Bishop Epiphanius of Salamis also declared that Mount Zion, which was once a privileged height, had now been 'cut off' (as heretical) from the rest of the church. This was the situation during the second half of the fourth century A.D.

To fend off Gentile influence, both pagan and Byzantine (that is, Gentile Christian), the Judeo-Christians of Mount Zion built a wall around their ancient sanctuary. It was this kind of ghetto wall that the Bordeaux Pilgrim referred to when he visited Mount Zion in 333 A.D. He entered and exited through a wall, he reported." [89]

The Catholic priest Ignazio Mancini, O.F.M., in his book *Archeological Discoveries Relative to the Judeo-Christians*, states: "... they started to disappear when what is called the "Great Church" began to make itself felt in Palestine. Their extinction was in sight when the new movement gained undisputed dominance ... It meant, first, the recision or cutting off of the Judao-Christians from the vital trunk of Christianity and, in the end, its total disappearance."[90]

"All these Councils from 380 on saw the hierarchy intent on eliminating the Church of the Circumcision, by now considered a source of heresy."[91]

Emanuel Testa, following in the footsteps of his colleague, Father Bellarmino Bagatti, O.F.M., documented the history of the final takeover of the original Jewish Apostolic Nazarenes by the Gentile church. Concerning the Byzantine building of a majestic basilica alongside the original Cenacle (throne of David) he writes: "In reality, those who were

---

[88] (from Pixner, footnote 37): the church fathers (Eusebius, Epipanius, Jerome and others) called it "a cottage in a cucumber field" (MPG 22, p. 43-44; Baldi, *Enchiridion*, nos. 733, 734

[89] This was the first ghettoization of the Jews under Roman Gentile Christianity. Many other calamities would befall the Jewish people at the hands of the Church as subsequent history has shown.

[90] Mancini, Ignazio, "*Archeological Discoveries Relative to the Judeo-Christians*," pages 173-174

[91] Emanuel Testa O.F.M., *the Faith of the Mother Church*, Franciscan Printing Press, Jerusalem Reprinted 1992. Pages 22-23

building a 'counter-altar' on Zion were not the Judeo-Christians who jealously preserved the old synagogue of the upper room, for many years the site of James' See, but the Byzantines of John II who, in 385, dedicated the sumptuous basilica of Holy Zion beside the Cenacle. In the criticized articles of faith as well, in Christology, in mariology, in sacramental matters, and in eschatology, the Judeo-Christians were not the ones who broke with tradition. It was the Councils which rejected their archaic forms in the name of the organic development of dogmas.

"It will be in the name of this organic evolution, assisted by the Holy Spirit, between August 386 and September 387, that Chrysostom, on orders from Bishop Flavian, will argue against the Judeo-Christians of Antioch in fully eight discourses even though he knew they were the ones faithful to the tradition. But by this time, 300 bishops, gathered at the Council of Nicea, with Christ Himself mystically present among them, have decided differently ... mindful therefore of condemning so many strong, wise fathers.

"In their name[92] they must give up defending Judiasim and believing that truth is on the side of the enemies of Christ[93] and disparaging the laws of the Church.

"The Old Law, in fact, is surpassed by the gospel; the synagogue is no longer a sacred place but a theater; circumcision is replaced by baptism; the Jewish Easter of 14 Nisan is realized in the Easter of Resurrection; the Temple, the priesthood, and the sacrifice have collapsed and been replaced by the priesthood of the Lord and his sacrificial crucifixion; the old Israel is now the Church; the source of salvation are the sacraments, no longer the witchcraft, spells, and anointings of healers who can cure the body but ruin the soul.

"Naught remains for all Judiazers but excommunication: "if the one who suffers from this illness is still a catechumen, let him be sent away from the vestibule of the church; if one of the faithful or an initiate, remove him from the Holy table.

"This harshness on the part of the hierarchy explains the interventions of civil authority against Jews in general and Judeo-Christians in particular; thus the prohibition against recurring to rabbinical tribunals, formerly highly regarded both for competence and superstition; the suppression of the synagogue's autonomy by law in 399; the removal by law in 418 of Jewish soldiers from the army; the

---

[92] By calling themselves Jewish Nazarenes and not Greek Christians.
[93] i.e., the Jews

prohibition against mixed marriages, made equal to adultery and therefore punishable by death."[94]

Epiphanius would have it that the throne of David had passed into the church. In his *Refutation of all Heresies*, he writes: "The Throne of David and the royal seat are the priesthood in the holy church, the very royal honor and High Priesthood which the Lord gave to his holy church which He himself united into one. He transferred the throne of David into the church, never to leave her."[95]

The Roman Catholic Church, which sits upon the seven hills of Rome, proclaimed herself directly descended from the Apostles. Following in a line of popes after Peter,[96] these antagonists of the original Nazarene movement thought to usurp the throne of David as the Hasmonian priest-kings had many centuries before.

Yet we find a different reality. In the upper room Synagogue over the tomb of their father David, a line of his descendants and of the family of Jesus their Messiah, guarded the royal throne and awaited the return of their master.

Let all those who would call themselves "Zionist" Christians[97] now, at the dawn of the third Millennium, find the true roots of their faith at the throne of David on Zion

---

[94] Emanuel Testa, O.F.M., *The Faith of the Mother Church*, pages 23-24

[95] Epiphanius, Bishop of Salamis (367-403) Panarion, Adversus Haereses

[96] It has always bothered me that Peter and the other principle Apostles and Nazarenes would not want to be buried on the Mount of Olives (like the Jews of all ages) in order to resurrect literally at the feet of their expected Messiah. Among the Judeo-Christian ossuaries excavated at Dominus Flavit on the Mount of Olives, one contained the Hebrew inscription "Sime'on Bar Jonah," Peter's proper name. F. Paul Peterson, in his book *Peter's tomb Recently Discovered in Jerusalem*, states that he had evidence that Franciscan Bagatti was convinced that he had found Peter's tomb (not in Rome) and charged that Pope Pius XII (IN 1953) had ordered this information suppressed.

[97] Hebrew: *Notzrim* (Shoots from the stump of Jesse). The early Jewish believers did not want to be called "Christians," a Greek appellation meaning "Messianics," but rather "Nazarenes" or "Shoots." This title was based upon the shoot" from the stump of Jesse" (or David) prophecies in the Bible. (Isaiah 11:1, Jer. 33:15, Zech. 6:12) As the Nazarenes saw it, the prophets had written that, at the advent of the Edenic age of righteousness, when the lion and the lamb would feed together, and pain and evil would cease and all of the remnant would return to the Land from all the lands to which they had been driven, that the House of David would again take root: "And a shoot goes out from the stump of Jesse, and a Branch (*Netzer*) will bear fruit out of his roots ... And it shall be in that day, the Root of Jesse stands as a banner of peoples; nations shall seek to him and his *resting place* (emphasis mine) shall be

41

glory....Cry and shout, O dweller of Zion! For great is the Holy One in your midst." (Isa 11:1, 10;12:6)

The biblical allegory of the stump of Jesse is the olive tree. This tree, common in Israel, can be cut down to the earth, killed by fire, or hollowed and rotted with advanced age, yet, at the scent of water it will shoot from its roots healthy and tender sprouts toward heaven. As can be seen in the Garden of Gethsemane, these seemingly-dying ancient trees can live for as many as 2,000 years. Though the trunk may die, yet the olive tree wages the ravages of time. The spark of life of the olive tree, more than any other tree, is in its root.

I must admit that in writing most of this article, I had missed a very important graffito connected with our artifacts. While sitting and carefully examining the pieces again, I made a stunning discovery. Besides the dominant Messianic Seal, there are other symbols on some of the pieces which I had earlier considered to be simple decoration. These other symbols are most definitely "olive shoots." Throughout Jewish history, the traditional symbol of the olive sprout has remained the same. The very symbol of the State of Israel is a candelabra bordered by two of these shoots. In my mind, it is certain that these "Nazarenes" considered their Messiah to have been the ultimate and first sprout from the ancient and long considered dead stump of Jesse from which they and many more sprouts would now spring forth.

The markings on one of our artifacts—a nearly complete oil lamp—to my mind, are very significant indeed. This piece, marked upon its spout from which the light once shown, with the Messianic Seal, sports around its oil well, twelve olive shoots. I believe that this is a clear statement of Nazarene beginnings; i.e., the Messiah and the original twelve apostles who were chosen by His hand. I contend that these Nazarenes believed that with the coming of their Messiah, the ancient stump of Jesse had sprouted anew from the dust at the throne of David on Zion. These pieces thus sport the two most important symbols for those who followed the house of David: the Star and the Shoot. Justin writes, "Another prophet, Isaiah, announces the same thing in other words.

A star will rise in Jacob and the flower will sprout on the stalk of Jesse, and the nations will hope in his arm. This bright star which rises, this flower on the stalk of Jesse is the Messiah." And again, in Revelations 22:16, another book of Judeo-Christian origin: "I am the root and the offspring of David, the bright morning star."

Then, going back to my source material (archeological evidence including Judeo-Christian graffito on Ossuaries, funerary stelae, amulets, etc.), I found that the Judeo Christians' were truly adamant in their insistence to be called "Shoots" and not "Messianics" and that this insistence is evident from the archeological record. In this graffito, olive shoots are strongly represented. The funerary stelae, amulets, and other soft stone objects, as well as oil lamps found at Khirbet Qilqish are literally plastered with shoots: straight, curved and crossed into a *Taw* which, with the Crucifixion, had taken on a new meaning. One graffito shows "living water," bordered by two vertical olive shoots.

After Word

I am convinced that a systematic study of the Dead Sea Scrolls, in their entirety, in this new light will validate the major thesis of these pages, of which some small part must for the present remain plausible conjecture. I happily accept any and all criticism or correction. My stated purpose, after all, is to get to the historical truth, as much as that is possible in historical hindsight, and fallible human endeavor.

My hope is that this will help to spark renewed research of the written word in manuscripts and scrolls and an archeological excavation of the catacombs of the Essene quarter of Mount Zion.

R.E.S.

Livnim, Israel

March 2, 1999

Let me conclude by quoting from Job (the broken), and the Psalms.

For there is hope of a tree, if it is cut down, that it will sprout again, and its shoot will not cease. Though its root becomes old in the earth, and its stump dies in the dust; yet at the scent of water it will bud, and bring forth branches like a plant." (Job 14:7-9)

You shall arise; have mercy on Zion; for the time to pity her, yea, the appointed time has come. For Your servants take pleasure in its stones, and pity its dust. So nations shall fear the name of the Lord, and all the kings of the earth Your glory. When the Lord shall build up Zion, He shall appear in His glory (Psalms 102:13-16, a Psalm of David.)

Part Two

An Interpretation of the
Biblical Meaning and Contemporary Significance
of the Messianic Seal of the Jerusalem Church

By
Raymond Robert Fischer

*Truth shall spring out of the earth, and righteousness
shall look down from heaven.* (Ps 85:11)

Introduction

I had the great pleasure and honor to be present with Reuven Schmalz and Ludwig Schneider in the library of the Schneiders' residence in Jerusalem during February 1999 and to participate in their discussions that provided the initiating basis for Reuven to record a summary of his long study in the foregoing historical account.

I am deeply impressed with the scholarship and thoroughness Reuven has provided as a background for our understanding of the many implications of the Messianic Seal of the Jerusalem Church. However, since Reuven intentionally and, I believe, necessarily approached this subject from a predominantly historical perspective, it has fallen on me to offer a further, more biblically oriented exposition, as well as my own understanding of the contemporary significance of this monumentally important discovery as it relates to Israel, the Church and the world beyond in these closing months of the second millennium.

Since, earlier this year, when I first beheld the Messianic Seal of the Jerusalem Church, etched and painted on the eight artifacts, I have continued to search for material facts— physically wandering around the site of the Messianic Synagogue on Mount Zion—literally digging my fingers into the ancient soil there in an effort to personally touch the reality of the place—all the while praying for divine guidance. I offer this personal insight with the hope the reader will understand that I don't, even for a moment, pretend to have all the answers or anything like a complete understanding of the Lord's purpose in all this. Simply, what understanding I have been given, I now joyfully share.

A Matter of Perspective

Since my own association with the Messianic Seal began, I have shared its amazing re-discovery with a number of friends and associates whose separate personal backgrounds and understandings generally fall within one or the other of two groups: Messianic Judaism,[98] or the many faceted, predominantly non-Jewish, world-wide Christian church.[99]

---

[98] Messianic Judaism is a biblically based movement of Jewish people who accept the truth that Yeshua (Jesus) is the promised Messiah of Israel. The current rapidly growing resurgence of what is, in effect, a modern day "shoot" from Nazarene Judaism, as it was practiced in the first synagogue on Mount Zion, can be traced to Great Britain where in 1813 a band of Jewish believers were united together in bonds of heritage, witnessing and relief as the "Hebrew Christian Alliance and Prayer Union of Great Britain." The movement

F. King David's Tomb on Mount Zion, situated immediately below the Upper Room. This was the site of the Jerusalem Church which was first pastored by James the Just, the brother of Jesus.

G. The seemingly dead stump of an ancient olive tree with many shoots springing up from its roots. Photographed in the Garden of Gethsemane. The Nazarenes, like their name implies, thought of themselves as "shoots" from the stump of Jesse.

H. The Upper Room on Mount Zion. About 25% of this structure is original, the rest has been rebuilt. This was the site of the Last Supper of Jesus, the gift of the Holy Spirit on Pentecost, and the location of the Jerusalem Church.

I. View from the roof of the Tomb of David/Upper Room on Mount Zion. The dome in the foreground is immediately above the Upper Room. The golden dome of the well known mosque on the Temple Mount can be seen in the distance at an elevation noticeably lower than the site of the Jerusalem Church on Mount Zion.

J. The formidable covering of the Ancient Grotto of the Jerusalem Church. This is where Tech Oteeoos found the eight artifacts in the 1960's. All remaining entrances to the Grotto were presumably covered soon after Ludwig Schneider was shown a perfect rendition of the Messianic Seal etched into stone wall some distance beyond the bottom of the seven cosmic stairs leading down into this ancient place of baptism.

K. Close-up photograph of the elaborate security measures taken to keep the curious from entering the ancient grotto of the Jerusalem Church.

L. Mosaic in the lower level of the Roman Catholic Church built adjacent to the Tomb (Throne) of David. The Madonna with child is shown standing upon the Throne of David which is depicted as the Stump of Jesse out of which is shown artist's conceptions of Mary's lineage leading to Jesus.

As each person, in turn, first excitedly examined photographs and reproductions taken from "strikes" of the artifacts, and then prayerfully considered the implications of what they had beheld, a number of different interpretations emerged as to how the message of the "Seal"

---

remained virtually dormant until the Arab-Israeli Six Day War in 1967, then it began to flourish. By the end of 1993 there were 165 independent Messianic Jewish congregations
world-wide. Today, there are an estimated 200 congregations, about fifty of which are in Israel, with the majority of the rest in the United States. The remainder are widely distributed throughout the rest of the world. There is a wide spectrum of doctrinal belief manifest in these groups, not unlike parallel and sometimes great differences in the non-Jewish church. Form and expression vary from very conservative to very liberal; from very Jewish to being almost indistinguishable from typically
non-Jewish; and from deeply fundamental to totally free charismatic. Even with these many diversities, most congregations share certain characteristics, such as: worship on the Sabbath, Davidic music and dance, and many other Jewish traditions consistent with biblical teachings. Membership is open to both Jews and Gentiles, and the membership of some congregations, especially in the United States, is predominantly Gentile.

Even with its continuing rapid growth, Messianic Judaism remains a very small group when compared to the whole of Judaism, while at the same time being overwhelmingly dwarfed by the relatively huge non-Jewish Christian church. There are just over 13 million Jews in the world: about 6 million each in both Israel and the United States. The other approximate one million are distributed in a continuing Diaspora that spans an additional 90 countries. For a number of reasons, it is difficult to accurately determine the number of ethnically Jewish Messianic believers among these 13 million total. For example, there are few membership roles in Israel where Messianic groups are openly opposed by their orthodox brothers who sometimes express their disagreement with stones and fire bombs. Even so, various estimates of the Messianic population show that there are about 4,000 to 5,000 Messianic Jews in Israel, and perhaps up to another 15,000 to 20,000 in the rest of the world. Even on the high side of these estimates, still less than two percent of world-wide Jews are believers in Yeshua; I believe that the actual number is probably much lower.

Then, consider even 25,000 Jewish believers, who, like a mere spark of light, are easily lost in the overwhelming shadow of their approximately two billion non-Jewish "Christian" brothers and sisters throughout the world, all grafted-in adherents to the very spiritual trunk that first "sprouted from the stump of Jesse" as a Jewish form of worship in the first Messianic Synagogue on Mount Zion.

[99] I mean to include here all groups (beyond those that identify themselves as "Messianic Jewish") who profess Jesus Christ as Lord and Savior and who otherwise hold to the basic Christian tenets commonly shared by the "universal" church.

should be understood. There were two areas of strong agreement and several other interpretations that seemed to be directly related to the greatly different historical, cultural, ethnic, spiritual backgrounds and worship practices of the individuals who were offering them.

The areas of agreement centered on two spiritual insights seen and shared by everyone who has beheld, then commented upon, the Messianic Seal.

The first of these commonly seen insights is that our Redeemer, the Son of God, who is usually worshipped as Yeshua haMaschiach by Messianic Jews, and who is more commonly known as Jesus Christ by non-Jewish believers, is absolutely central to each of the three separate elements of the Messianic Seal while, at the same time, being the very essence of its total meaning.

The second universally perceived insight is that there is a strong message of unity, seen variously at several different levels and in several different ways, inherent in and proclaimed by the three separate elements as they make up the totality of the "Seal."

It has become apparent to many who have offered an interpretation of the "Seal," that, first, it is a divinely inspired mirror image of the Trinity, and second, its three parts, while distinctly separate, make up a wonderful unity (*Echad*), itself joyfully crying out the words of the *Shema*: "Hear, O Israel: The LORD our God, the LORD is one![100]

Each member of the Trinity has its own specific identity and function. In the same way Messianic Judaism and the Gentile Christian church have different identities, practices and traditions, yet together they *should* make up a wonderful unity that is the universal church.

Sadly, the history of the early church up to the year 400 CE, and the following events of ecclesiastical history even until today, have too often been divisive with the result that Messianic Judaism quickly became and has remained generally isolated from the very Gentile church to which it gave birth—seemingly torn asunder by a whole bag full of tricks orchestrated by the enemy, Satan himself.

In order to offer a proper interpretation of the meaning of the Messianic Seal, I believe it is first necessary to show, as a basis for healing and restoration, where these points of division have occurred and remain between Messianic Judaism and the Gentile church. It is my heartfelt desire that once these points of division are understood, all believers, working together can tear down the barriers thus identified and

---

[100] Deut. 6:4

work towards a reconciled universal church that will at last stand in blessed unity.

I believe it is for this very purpose that the Lord has once again brought forth the Messianic Seal after nearly 2,000 years of suppression. I feel certain that His purpose is for us to first understand the wonderful message of unity implicit in this ancient symbol, and then, by His very Hand, He will write it upon each of our hearts.

It is with these different perspectives in mind that I offer my own interpretation. Let me quickly say that I don't pretend to represent all of my Israeli Messianic brethren with this offering. There is much truth in the old adage that where two Jews are gathered together, there are at least three opinions; so it goes as well with doctrinal positions and interpretations. Thus, this is my personal view: nothing more.

Mt. Zion and the Temple Mount

As a point of departure, I believe it is important to set aside what I believe is a misconception, commonly held throughout the church, that "Jerusalem," "The Temple," "Mount Zion," and "Zion," as they are frequently referenced throughout Scripture, are all the same geographical location. That the frequent use of "Zion" should always be understood as a euphemism meaning "Jerusalem," and/or the "Temple," is, I believe, an error, easily demonstrated by both geographic realities and the Scriptures themselves.

The well-understood geographic and historical realities are that the three Jewish Temples[101] were each, in turn, located near the top of Mount Moriah, more commonly known as the Temple Mount.[102] Where these Jewish Temples once stood proudly, right above the remnants of the Western (Wailing) Wall, stand today two Mosques in what was once an exclusively Jewish holy place. As Reuven pointed out in the foregoing

---

[101] The Third Temple, built by Herod, was actually a major expansion if not a complete re-building of the second Temple, thus, there is often confusion since some commentators refer to just two Temples, not three, in that they combine the second and third Temples into a single reference.
[102] "Temple" (Article: from Nelson's Illustrated Bible Dictionary) (Copyright (C) 1986, Thomas Nelson Publishers) Electronic Database Copyright (C) 1996 by Biblesoft)

historical account, when the paganistic Hasmonean presence took over "management" of the Holy of Holies in the Third Temple, the spiritual lights literally went out of the place, and they haven't since been rekindled.

Jerusalem is situated on five hills. One of these, identified by Josephus as the "Third Hill," is also known as Mount Moriah, the site of the three Jewish Temples. Outside of both the ancient and current walls of the Old City, and several hundred meters to the South, at a noticeably higher elevation, lies what Josephus called the "Western Hill," or, more commonly, "Mount Zion."[103] This, I believe, has convincingly been established by Reuven and others as the location of David's Tomb.

I believe it isn't a long reach to suggest that when the spiritual lights were turned off in the now desecrated Third Temple, they were soon turned back on with glaring brilliance, just up hill on the adjacent ridge in the Messianic synagogue built astride the tomb of King David, and to further suggest the "hand" that threw the switch, thus inaugurating and illuminating His beautiful, new, at first all-Jewish bride, belonged to Yeshua, the Son of God, our Redeemer, the long-awaited Jewish Messiah.

The Temple Mount and Mount Zion are two distinctly separate places with distinctly different attachments. The first, both historically and spiritually, is melded with the Old Covenant; the second, with the New Covenant.

In the Old Testament (NKJV) there are 19 specific references to "Mount Zion" and 144 to simply "Zion." In the New Testament (NKJV) there are two specific references to "Mount Zion" and seven to simply "Zion."

I wouldn't begin to argue that none of these references were euphemisms for "Jerusalem." Clearly, at least several of them in the Old Testament are such. However, I would suggest that many of them (at least several in the Old Testament and perhaps all in the New) are specific references to the geographic site and/or the eschatological importance of the location of the first Messianic Synagogue; i.e., Mount Zion.

For example:

For out of Jerusalem shall go a remnant, and those who escape from Mount Zion. The zeal of the LORD of hosts will do this.' [104] *(II Ki 19:31)*

---

[103] Josephus, WARS, Book 5: Chapter 4, (143) "Jerusalem"
[104] Mount Zion is spoken of as a separate place from Jerusalem

Then the moon will be disgraced and the sun ashamed; for the LORD of hosts will reign on Mount Zion and in Jerusalem and before His elders, gloriously.[105] (Isa 24:23)

"But on Mount Zion there shall be deliverance, and there shall be holiness; the house of Jacob shall possess their possessions."[106] (Obad. 17)

Therefore it is also contained in the Scripture, (Isa 28:16) "Behold, I lay in Zion a chief cornerstone, elect, precious, and he who believes on Him will by no means be put to shame."[107](1 Pet 2:6)

Then I looked, and behold, a Lamb standing on Mount Zion, and with Him one hundred and forty-four thousand, having His Father's name written on their foreheads.[108] (Rev 14-1)

The Messianic Synagogue on Mount Zion

The Movement (Messianic Judaism) headed[109] by James (the brother of Jesus)[110] from the 40s to the 60s CE in Jerusalem with the Temple

---

[105] Allah, the god of the Mosques on the Temple Mount, as is commonly misunderstood, is not considered by Islam, Judaism or Christianity to be the same God worshipped commonly by Jews and Christians; i.e., YHWH. The prophet shows Yeshua reigning from both Mount Zion and Jerusalem (two distinct places.)

[106] This would seem to be a clear prophecy foretelling the reign of King Yeshua from Mount Zion (Rev. 14:1)

[107] An obvious reference to Yeshua (see Romans 9:32-33)

[108] The returning King Yeshua will be seated upon and reign from His rightful place, the Throne of David, which sprang as a shoot from Jesse on the top of Mount Zion.

[109] "In the traditions recorded by Eusebius (Hegesippus, Clement of Alexandria, Origen) James was the first bishop of the Jerusalem church. His election to this position is located at the beginning of the life of the Jerusalem church ...." Painter, John, *Just James*, Page 4

The account of the Jerusalem assembly (Acts 15:13) portrays James 'presiding,' and this position of leadership is consistent with the remainder of the narrative of Acts. Additional scriptures giving testimony to James' position as leader of the church are: Acts 12:17 (Peter reports his experience through "channels" thus the inference that James is in authority), Acts 21:18 (James is sought out as the obvious leader of the elders), 1Cor 15:4-8 (Among the hierarchy, Yeshua appeared first to Peter, then to James, then to Paul; a tradition holds that this post-resurrection appearance of Yeshua to his brother James was the genesis of James' conversion and hence the basis for his appointment to the leadership of the Jerusalem Church); Gal. 1:18-19 (Paul confirms that the man in charge whom he saw was James).

still standing, was the principal one of a number of *minim* (Jewish sects) as categorized in the Talmud.[111]

The upper room, as it has mostly been rebuilt,[112] can still be seen today on Mount Zion where it is located directly above the Tomb of David. This was the site of several epochal events in early church history, most notably the Last Supper,[113] the gathering place where the disciples went after Yeshua's ascension,[114] and the place where the Holy Spirit came upon them at Pentecost.[115]

The upper room, large enough to easily hold 120 persons, was in every sense a synagogue dedicated to the worship of Yeshua: a place for the reading of scripture, for instruction, for the taking of the Lord's Supper; to wit, the evolving site where first occurred the institutionalized worship of Yeshua haMashiach. It is also presumed that James actually lived at this location.[116]

With the rapid early growth of the body of believers in Jerusalem,[117] the Messianic synagogue, quartered in the upper room, presumably, very early in its existence, was unable to accommodate the rapidly increasing number of new believers. Accordingly, new spin off Messianic Jewish groups, extending from the Mount Zion assembly, met regularly in the Temple courts, in other synagogues, and in private homes where they

---

[110] There has been a relatively recent voluminous and excellent addition to the body of historical writing dedicated to James the brother of Jesus. (this blood relationship/kinship is referred to specifically in Gal. 1:19, Matt. 13:55 and Mark 6:3) That Mary and Joseph had other children following the birth of Yeshua is additionally attested to or can be inferred from: Matt. 12:46, Mark 3:31, Luke 8:19, John 2:12, John 7:3, Acts 1:14, 1Cor. 9:5, Luke2:7, Matt. 1:25, Matt. 27:56 and Mark 15:40. For an exhaustive study of James, I commend the reader to the two most recent works on this subject: Eisenman, Robert, *James the Brother of Jesus*, Penguin Books, New York 1998, 1074 pages; and, Painter, John, *Just James, The Brother of Jesus in History and Tradition*, University of South Carolina Press, Columbia, 1997, 326 pages
[111] Eisenman, Robert, *James the Brother of Jesus*, page 5
[112] Bagatti, B., *The Church from the Circumcision*, page 119
[113] Mark 14:15-16
[114] Acts 1:11-13
[115] Acts 2:1-13
[116] Bagatti, B. "*The Church from the Circumcision*," pp. 116-117
[117] Acts 2:47

broke bread together.[118] At these public worship services, teachings and a witness in the name of Yeshua were offered to all within reach. [119]

The scriptures give us considerable insight into the worship practices of these early Messianic Jewish synagogues: prayer was offered, not only on Shabbat, but on special occasions as well,[120] and Scripture[121] was read.[122]

The breaking of bread and the sharing of the cup were observed as a continuing proclamation of Yeshua's death, an anticipation of His return, and a participation in His body and blood. Offerings for the needy were also received .

Father Bagatti has provided us with a fascinating and detailed description of how the sacrament of baptism was administered in the Sacred Grotto near the upper room.[123]

---

[118] Acts 2:46   Perhaps a first reference to "home communion."

[119] Lockyear, Herbert, Sr., " Church: Its Use in the New Testament," *Nelson's Bible Dictionary*. Thomas Nelson Publishers, 1986, Electronic Database, Biblesoft, 1996

[120] Acts 12:5

[121] The Bible of the early Jewish believers on Mount Zion consisted of the Old Testament writings, and the "Gospel According to the Hebrews," which was an early version of the Gospel According to Matthew with which it is believed to have borne an almost exact resemblance. For an excellent discussion of the Gospel According to the Hebrews, see: Pritz, Ray A., *Nazarene Jewish Christianity*: The Magnes Press, The Hebrew University, Jerusalem-Leiden , 1988, Chapter 6 (all). Interestingly, history has recorded that a copy of the Gospel According to the Hebrews, was found in the tomb of Barnabus on Cyprus around 400 CE, but then unexplainably again vanished from sight. While it cannot be certain, I believe it is also likely that the Nazarenes had access to at least several other early New Testament writings.

[122] James 1:22

[123] Bagatti, paraphrasing St. Cyril and Egeria, (both Church Fathers) : "[Those to be baptized] were introduced into the atrium of the baptistery, where, facing the West they renounced Satan, and then facing the East they made a profession of faith with the recital of the creed. Then, each one, divesting [undressing], was anointed with exorcised oil, and then they entered the baptismal basin, immersing themselves three times [in the manner of a ritual Jewish *mikvah* purification rite] ... for the women it seems it was the custom for deaconesses ... to assist [in order to hide] from the gaze of the curious the body of the female being baptized. In fact they [the male officiates] did not carry out any ceremony, much less the anointing with oil of exorcism, since this obliged the baptizer to touch the whole body." See: Bagatti, B., *The Church from the Gentiles in Palestine*, Jerusalem, Franciscan Printing Press, 1984, p.303.
As a matter for further speculation, the traditional Jewish *mikvah* purification rite involves seven successive self-immersions. It would seem an easy reach to describe this shortened (three immersion) Messianic Jewish baptism as a

52

One might ask: How could *any* of these Nazarene beliefs and worship practices be more perfectly in agreement with today's mainstream non-Jewish Christianity?

Unity in Yeshua—Not Uniformity

There was then and remains today what should be an untroubling distinction between Messianic Judaism and the non-Jewish Christian church whose scions were soon to be grafted in among the natural Jewish shoots, waiting and receptive to henceforth share nourishment from their own precious common root who, by His own proclamation, was, is, and ever more shall be Yeshua, the promised and come Messiah.

---

touching obedient reply of these first on-fire believers in Yeshua literally fulfilling the Great Commission (Matt 28:19) "... baptizing them in the name of the Father and of the Son and of the Holy Spirit ... ."

Emmanuel Testa, O.F.M., in his book, *The Faith of the Mother Church*, pages 146-154, using Cyril of Jerusalem and other church fathers as his source, offers further details of the Nazarene baptismal rite. He suggests that the entire ceremony including the full body anointing with oil, the three, separate, full body immersions in water, together with the accompanying confessions, professions and liturgy, in sum represent three different baptisms: the Baptism of Fire, the Baptism of Water, and the Baptism of the Spirit.

The Baptism of Fire was the first of the three "rites." The persons to be baptized were instructed on the doctrine of the Way of light (Essene rooted), then many symbolical lamps were lit to brilliantly illuminate the Grotto. One can easily imagine the officiate proclaiming from the just penned Gospel of John, "I am the Light of the world ... ." Interestingly, one of our artifacts recovered in this very place is a small Roman lamp, decorated with both the "Messianic Seal"and many "shoots." I feel certain that it was used in many of these Baptisms of Fire.

The second rite, I would suggest, centered on the three separate immersions "... in the name of the Father, and the Son and the Holy Spirit."

The third "rite" was Baptism of the Spirit, suggested by Cyril to represent that part of Yeshua's baptism when He was filled with the Holy Spirit, symbolized by the dove that rested upon Him. I would further suggest that this was the Pentecostal "Baptism of the Holy Spirit," which provided an appropriate spiritually charged finale to this incredibly meaningful and exciting initiation of the new believers into "born-again" membership of the Body.

53

"... I am the Root and the Offspring of David, and the bright Morning Star[124].

This singular distinction, I believe, is the common genesis of the de-Judaizing compulsion of Constantine and his exclusively Gentile church fathers, the prevalent error of replacement theology which holds that biblical Israel has been replaced by the church itself, and the bitter root of anti-Semitism, both historic and contemporary, that fanned the flames of the Holocaust, the Crusades, and all the rest; and even today, with ever growing fervor and increasing world-wide support, seemingly still seeks to destroy both the Nation and the State of Israel.

This important distinction between the Jewish and Gentile "branches" of the church is the unalterable position of Jewish believers that their Messiah Yeshua meant what He said when He proclaimed to all Jews, believers and unbelievers alike:

"Do not think that I came to destroy the Law or the Prophets. I did not come to destroy but to fulfill. For assuredly, I say to you, till heaven and earth pass away, one jot or one tittle will by no means pass from the law till all is fulfilled. Whoever therefore breaks one of the least of these commandments, and teaches men so, shall be called least in the kingdom of heaven; but whoever does and teaches them, he shall be called great in the kingdom of heaven." [125]

---

[124] Rev. 22:16

[125] Matt. 5:17-19 This teaching was part of the Sermon on the Mount (Matt 5:17-19) presented by Yeshua to Great multitudes (that) followed Him—from Galilee, and from Decapolis, Jerusalem, Judea, and beyond the Jordan. (Matt 4:25) It is interesting to note that all of these places were Nazarene centers. Yeshua was therefore preaching essentially to those future Nazarene sect adherents who would soon build the first Messianic synagogue on Mount Zion. These were the same Nazarenes that would later stand and watch with awe as Yeshua ascended into heaven, and then were properly identified by two angels as "men of Galilee." As was His regular practice, just as He taught the Jews in their synagogues, He was now speaking to great crowds of Jews from these predominantly Nazarene Jewish communities. While there may have been some Gentiles in the crowd, they were clearly in a small minority. Why would Yeshua be teaching Gentiles about the Law of Moses when they would have had absolutely no familiarity with this Law and wouldn't have in any way understood what He was talking about?

"Jewish believers are not saved by their adherence to the Law; however, contrary to popular opinion in the church, they are told nowhere in the New Testament to abandon it. They are in fact, not given 'liberty' to do so, any more than non-Jewish 'Christians' are given the liberty to disregard what the Torah says about moral behavior. Therefore, maintenance of Jewish identity is not a casual option of no consequence for Jewish believers: it is a biblical incumbency of serious import." (Rabbi Bruce L. Cohen from: "Why Messianic Judaism?" p.2

That there is a Holy-Spirit orchestrated distinction between Jewish and Gentile believers seems clearly evident from both Scripture and history. Yeshua Himself was Torah observant as were and remained all twelve apostles and all the Nazarenes: so are most contemporary Jewish believers who, to varying degrees, keep Torah. Any dispensational argument that the Torah somehow became irrelevant with the resurrection of Yeshua breaks down in the light of Scripture. To be sure, Gentiles are informed that they too, in perpetuity, remain under four specific Torah legislated requirements.[126]

Scripture teaches that the Torah will continue to be observed even unto and in the "New Temple Era,"[127] (interpreted by many commentators to be the millennial church) wherein, among other Torah observances, Jewish feasts will continue to be kept.[128]

There is a perfect harmony between the teachings of Yeshua and His Apostles—they all agree upon this point: Jewish believers are not to cease observing what Torah is possible to observe, and they are not to abandon their Jewish culture for another culture when they are "born again" in Yeshua. On the other hand, Gentile believers are under no parallel obligation to observe Torah except as specifically required by Scripture.[129] They are in no way obligated to abandon their own culture to adopt all or part of the Jewish culture, but they are free to do so if they so desire.[130]

The Heart of the Problem: Different Interpretations

The church fathers evidently had a different view of what Yeshua taught in His Sermon on The Mount about the Law[131] and how it

---

[126] Acts 15:20
[127] Eziekiel 40:1-4
[128] Zech 14:16, Ezek 46
[129] Acts 15:20
[130] Cohen, Rabbi Bruce, "Why Messianic Judaism," page 3
[131] In the Hebrew (more accurately Aramaic) spoken by Yeshua, the word Torah is more properly translated "teaching" or "instruction" as opposed to "law" in the sense of legislative law. In the New Testament, however, nomos, the Greek word used for "law" is properly translated in the harsher sense of "legislative law." A great havoc of misunderstanding has arisen from this subtle linguistic distinction. Remember, Matthew was originally written in Hebrew (Aramaic), the language Yeshua used when He presented the Sermon on the Mount. He

applied to Jews. They were seemingly utterly perplexed, and saw heresy in the notion that a Jew could still remain obedient to the Torah and at the same time be saved.

The church father Jerome, writing in the fourth century described the Nazarenes as those "...who accept Christ in such a way that they do not cease to observe the old Law."[132] Epiphanius, another fourth century church father and detractor of the sect of Jewish believers offers, in part, the following:

"But these sectarians did not call themselves Christians—but 'Nazarenes.' However, they are simply complete Jews. They use not only the New Testament but the Old Testament as well, as the Jews do—They have no different ideas, but confess everything exactly as the Law proclaims it and in the Jewish fashion—except for their belief in Christ, if you please! For they acknowledge both the resurrection of the dead and the divine creation of all things, and declare that God is one, and that His son is Jesus Christ—They are different from Jews, and different from Christians, only in the following. They disagree with Jews because they have come to faith in Christ; but since they are still fettered by the Law—circumcision, the Sabbath, and the rest—they are not in accord with Christians—they are nothing but Jews! They have the Gospel according to Matthew in its entirety in Hebrew. For it is clear that they still preserve this, in the Hebrew alphabet, as it was originally written."[133]

The Apostle Paul made several assertions in his epistles that, at first glance, seem to contradict Yeshua's seemingly clear imperative concerning Torah, as recorded in two gospels,[134] wherein Yeshua (speaking in Hebrew) proclaimed that Torah, i.e., the "teaching" or "instruction" of the Old Covenant has always applied to Jews and it will continue to do so.

Gentile Christian church theologians tend to exegete these Pauline teachings to arrive at the position that Yeshua had come to fulfill the Law, and, by so doing, had simultaneously abolished it, thus freeing Jews from their burdensome yoke of all things Jewish by canceling any and all obligations; i.e., ceremonial law, (the keeping of Shabbat, celebrating the feasts, the Abrahamic Covenant requiring circumcision, the inheritance of the Land of Israel for "a thousand generations," etc.)

---

was talking about "Law" in the Hebrew/Aramaic ("teaching/instruction") sense of *Torah*, not in the Greek sense of "legalism."
[132] Jerome: In his writings on Isaiah 8:14 as quoted by Pritz, p 58.
[133] Epiphanius: from "Panarion" 29 Quoted from an article, *What is Nazarene Judaism?* By James Trimm and Chris Lingle, The Society for the Advancement of Nazarene Judaism, (www.Nazarene.net) page 1
[134] Matt 5: 17-19 and Luke 16:17.

leaving in force only the moral law; as it was given to Moses (the Ten Commandments, etc.)

The most extreme of these interpreters, such as Epiphanius, have even suggested that *everything* Jewish had been set aside, to include culturally distinctive traditions, even the Hebrew language in so far as it was used to record Scripture.

The epistle references most often brought into play on these points are found in Galatians 3, Ephesians 2, and Romans 10.

Dr. Ray Pritz, a Gentile church-rooted biblical scholar and theologian who has lived in Israel for many years, offers:

"The parting of the ways [between the Nazarenes and the church fathers] is at the Law of Moses. It is their [the Nazarenes'] observance of the Law—and this alone—which, for Epiphanius, separates the Nazarenes from the main Church. 'Only in this respect they differ from the ... Christians.' It is this one thing which so stands out that it is essentially the only thing remembered by subsequent Fathers against the sect ... It makes little difference that the first Jewish believers continued to keep the Law (Acts 15; 21:20-26); it is immaterial that the epistle to the Galatians was addressed to Christians from *gentile* background or that Paul perhaps never wrote against *Jewish* Christians keeping the Law. The significance of all of this has long since been lost to men like Epiphanius. The Law is taboo. (from p.45)

"To attempt to keep it is to put oneself under a curse. If the Nazarenes want to observe parts of the Law, then they are 'Jews and nothing else.' Never mind if the same could be said for James or Peter, or indeed Paul. [all of whom, as well as the others of the original Twelve were strict keepers of Torah][135] For our purposes, ... here we have a body of Jewish believers who have managed to preserve the very earliest traditions of their forebears." [136]

While it isn't surprising that Dr. Pritz and others may sometimes quarrel with the more extreme interpreters of Paul's writings, it does seem remarkable to me that even Peter, his fellow apostle, found Paul's writings difficult to interpret:

Therefore, beloved, looking forward to these things, be diligent to be found by Him in peace, without spot and blameless; and account that the long

---

[135] Paul (and presumably the other Apostles) found it necessary to hurry back to Jerusalem to be present there to celebrate the three annual feasts as mandated by the Ceremonial Law of Moses.
See: (for example) Acts 18:19-21, 20:6, 20:16
[136] Pritz, Ray A., *Nazarene Jewish Christianity*, Jerusalem-Leiden: The Magnes Press, 1988, pp.44-45

suffering of our Lord is salvation— as also our beloved brother Paul, according to the wisdom given to him, has written to you, as also in all his epistles, speaking in them of these things, in which are some things hard to understand, which untaught and unstable people twist to their own destruction, as they do also the rest of the Scriptures.[137]

Messianic Rabbi Bruce Cohen, leader of a large New York Messianic Congregation, respected teacher, author and theologian, zeros in on what he sees as the very genesis of the multiple tragedies and misunderstandings that have befallen the Nazarene believers and their Messianic progeny:

"The primary error ... is well embodied by the standard view of certain passages in the book of Galatians ... Paul writes to address a problem: some misinformed Jewish believers from Israel visited Galatia and told the non-Jewish Galatian believers that if they did not become Jews by circumcision and by practice of the entire Torah, they were not truly saved (Acts 15:24) ....

"However, to apply this edict concerning Gentiles to the Jewish people is to entirely ignore the rest of Galatians, as well as the rest of the New Testament! Galatians 3:28 is often misapplied by reciting the first part of it, and not examining its entire sense: 'There is (in the New Testament dispensation) neither Jew nor Greek ... is chanted to say that there are now no differences between Jew and Gentile, and that all differences in religious practice and national identity should therefore be done away with. Yet the passage does not end there.

"It goes on to say '... there is neither slave nor free, there is neither male nor female; for you are all one in Christ Jesus.'... Galatians is not saying that these differences no longer exist or have meaning in the real world [there are indeed obvious differences between male and female, etc.] ... Paul was writing that these things mean nothing with regard to how a person gets saved! Jew, Greek, master, worker, male, female all get saved the same way: by repenting from sin and turning in faith to God to receive atonement through the finished work of Yeshua the Messiah. Galatians [and the other Pauline writings that speak to this point] does not teach that Jewishness is wrong or bad. It teaches that non-Jews are not required to adopt the mandates upon the Jewish people in order to receive salvation."[138]

[137] 2Peter 3:14-16
[138] Cohen, Rabbi Bruce L., *Why Messianic Judaism?*: Congregation Beth El of Manhattan, p.6

Dr. David H. Stern, the pre-eminent Messianic theologian and author, provides an exhaustive treatment of these Pauline passages in his *Jewish New Testament Commentary*, a very brief summary of which is:

"... One could understand the passage [Ephesians 2:15] to be saying that for His body, the Messianic Community, Yeshua abolished not the *Torah* in its entirety, but the *takkanot* (rabbinical ordinances) relating to the separation of Jews and Gentiles spiritually. The middle wall of the spiritual temple is done away with forever."[139]

Then, Dr. Stern separately continues:

"Consider Romans 10:4, which states—in a typical but wrong translation—"For Christ ends the law and brings righteousness for everyone who has faith." Like this translator, most theologians understand the verse to say that Yeshua terminated the *Torah*. But the Greek word translated 'ends' is *telos*, ... the normal meaning of *telos* ...which is also its meaning here ... is "goal, purpose, consummation," not "termination." The Messiah did not and does not bring the *Torah* to an end. "Rather, attention to and faith in the Messiah is the goal and purpose toward which the Torah aims, the logical consequence, result and consummation of observing the *Torah* out of genuine faith, as opposed to trying to observe it out of legalism. This is not the termination of *Torah*, is Paul's point, as can be seen from the context of Romans 9:30-10:11."[140]

The Nazarenes of Mount Zion, like their contemporary Messianic Jewish progeny, elected to keep their Jewish religious and cultural identities because they were and are convinced that this is what both the Old and New Testaments require of them. The Jewish Messiah did not come to save Jews from their Jewishness: He came to save them, and all mankind from its sin.[141]

Today, in a grassy, shaded area less than one hundred meters behind the still partly ancient building that houses the Tomb of David and the upper room, stands a large circa first century CE grotto, forbiddingly encased in a heavy-gauge steel mesh cage-like cover, its only remaining entrance painstakingly secured by multiple heavy chains and a large brass lock.

Looking through the steel mesh one can see the traditional seven cosmic stairs leading down to an ancient Jewish *mikva* (place for

---

[139] Stern, David H., *Jewish New Testament Commentary*, Clarksville, Maryland: Jewish New Testament Publications, Inc., 1996, page 588
[140] Stern, Dr. David H., *Messianic Jewish Manifesto*, Jerusalem, Jewish New Testament Publications, 1988, pp 127-128
[141] Cohen, Bruce, page 6

ceremonial cleansing, and in this case, for the Nazarene practice of anointing with oil as a preliminary to water and Spirit baptisms).

Beyond the *mikva* can be seen the beginning of a catacomb that soon vanishes from sight behind its first bend. According to the testimony of Elisheva Schmalz (wife of Reuven) this catacomb splits off and runs in many directions crisscrossing the entire area under Mount Zion, a "secret" place of childhood adventure she frequently visited with her young girlhood friends (circa 1962-1967). These journeys into (under) "no-man's land" (the children entered through a hidden cave mouth on the Israeli border) were extremely dangerous, to say the least.

According to the testimony of Ludwig Schneider, in 1994, on one of the walls near the bottom of this *mikva*, just before the first bend, Tech Oteeoos, his ancient monk friend and benefactor, pointed out to him a "perfect rendition of the three-part symbol etched into the stone."

Ludwig further testifies that in his continuing excitement, after he and Tech Oteeoos had parted, he went to the nearby monastery to report his find to some appropriate official. Instead of being welcomed as he had hoped, he was greeted rudely by the monk who answered the door, and even after explaining his purpose, was commanded to leave. The elaborate security measures taken to secure the grotto were presumably implemented soon after Ludwig's encounter at the monastery.

The Meaning of the Messianic Seal of the Jerusalem Church
The Sum of Its Parts

From the moment I first beheld this incredible three-part symbol, my head was filled with all manner of various interpretations. While many of these first and later thoughts were essentially speculative, at least some of them, I believe, were inspired by the Holy Spirit as equipage for the task at hand.

Therefore, despite the great temptation to do otherwise, I offer herewith only such interpretation that I have been able to support with Scripture, and/or credible extra-Scriptural sources. It is my prayerful hope that the reader will use these interpretations as a basis for their own edification, further study and unrestrained private speculation.

Many will remember the mathematical axiom: "The whole is equal to the sum of its parts." So, in my view, is this a proper interpretation of the meaning of the Messianic Seal.

Thus, as a starting point in seeking to understand the meaning of the entire Messianic Seal, we should, I believe, first examine the three distinctly separate symbols: the Menorah, the Star of David, and the fish from which it is comprised.

Then, we will also examine the use of the Hebrew letter *taw* as it clearly appears on one of the artifacts as the eye of the fish, and may also have been used in the same way on a second artifact.

Finally, we will consider the clear possibility that the Nazarenes deliberately included the six points of the Star of David as perfect renditions of the ancient Hebrew letter *Aleph*, and the most interesting and exciting implications of such a possible inclusion.

The Menorah

The original menorah was made according to *YHWH*'s precise instructions[142] to light the inside of the Tabernacle. Approximately 1.5 meters high and 1 meter across the top, made of fine gold, it was placed on the south wall of the Holy Place, to the right of the altar, and on the opposite side of the table. Its seven olive-oil lamps were lit each day at twilight and filled each morning.[143]

In biblical times, three successive temples were built on the same site: Solomon's, Zerubbabel's, and Herod's. Solomon built the First Temple on the east side of "... Jerusalem on Mount Moriah, where *the* LORD had appeared to his father David, at the place that David had prepared, on the threshing floor of Ornan the Jebusite." [144]

Seven menorahs adorned the Holy Place of Solomon's Temple, and since these seven original menorahs could not be found, only one menorah, representing the seven, was placed in the Holy Place of Zerubbabel's (Second)Temple. Following the precedent of the Second Temple, the Holy Place of Herod's (Third) Temple was also illuminated by only one menorah.

The single menorah that survived to illuminate the Second Temple, then the Herodian Temple, was next taken by Titus and carried, in his triumph, to Rome where it was deposited as a "trophy" in the "Temple of Peace." Genseric, 400 years later, transferred the singular menorah to Carthage. Next, Belisarius recovered it and carried it to Constantinople, after which, in 533 CE it was transferred back to Jerusalem and there

---

[142] Exodus 25:31-40
[143] Exodus 30:7-8
[144] II Chron. 3:1 (NASV)

deposited with the now Gentile church. It has never since been heard of or seen.[145]

Because this one, surviving menorah was an obvious symbolic representation of all things Jewish, one could surmise that it met with the same fate, administered by the same hands, as did the Messianic Seal with which it was so graciously adorned. Like the "Seal," the menorah may have been subscribed to oblivion, but unlike the "Seal," the menorah has not yet reemerged.

Today, from its divine rooting in the second book of Torah, the menorah has become the official symbol of the State of Israel, but more poignantly, it remains the spiritual and very national life symbol of the Nation of Israel, and of Judaism itself.[146]

"Variations are found in synagogues throughout the world, and the design rivals the six pointed star for popularity as a Jewish symbol."[147] All Jews, in Israel and throughout the continuing Diaspora, religious, Messianic, and secular alike, hold this symbol as something deeply sacred.

A Symbolic Representation of *YHWH*:   I would suggest that the menorah is first, a symbolic representation of *YHWH*, the God of Abraham, Isaac and Jacob:

- It is made of pure gold, symbolizing preciousness, sacredness and incorruptibility, all of which are characteristics of God.[148] It has seven branches, a mystical number implying divine perfection.

- It was to burn always while the Temple stood,[149] and spiritually, as an eternal light unto the world, long after the man made temples

---

[145] Fausset, Robert A., "The Golden Candlestick," *Fausset's Bible Dictionary*, Grand Rapids: Zondervan, 1949

[146] Father Bagatti, discussing the church father Jerome's comments about the menorah's use by Jews in their celebration of the Feast of Tabernacles, writes, " In reality for many centuries the candelabrum has been a symbol of the Jewish people, but in ancient times it was common also among the Judaeo-Christians...."Jerome writes, that"... The candelabrum was held as an indispensable element of the festive stage. It had the signification of the light and of the tree of life, which turned about the number seven: seven branches, seven days of the creation, seven months etc...." See: Bagatti, B., *"The Church from the Circumcision,"* page 202. It should also be observed that the "Tree of Life," lies at the very center of Essene theology and worship practice. See: Szekely, Edmond. B., *The Teachings of the Essenes From Enoch To the Dead Sea Scrolls*, Saffron Walden,: C.W. Daniel Co., 1988, page 51

[147] Stern, David H., *Jewish New Testament Commentary*, p. 692

[148] Exodus 25:31-39

[149] Exodus 27:20

were turned to dust, as evidenced by its presence in Zechariah's vision, and in John's Revelation.[150]

- In the scriptures, *YHWH* is frequently associated with light. Thus, there is an obvious association following, linking *YHWH* with the Menorah from which His sacred light illuminated the Holy Place in the Temple and continues to spiritually illuminate the world. For example: "... God is light; ..."[151] and, the "... Father of lights..."[152] God is further described as "He wraps himself with light as with a garment."[153] [He] alone possesses immortality and dwells in unapproachable light ..."[154]

A Symbolic Representation of Yeshua: Beyond the obvious truth that every association of the menorah with the Father is also an association of it with His Son,[155] there are many direct scriptural associations of the menorah with Yeshua.[156]

- While the menorah is not the light, it bears the *Light* for the illumination of all. Yeshua declared Himself to be "the *Light* of the World."[157]

---

[150] Zech. 4:2, Rev. 1:12
[151] 1John 1:5 (NASV)
[152] James 1:17 (NASV)
[153] Psalms 104:2 (NIV)
[154] 1 Tim. 1:16 (NASV)
[155] John 10:30
[156] The following scriptures refer to Yeshua as the light or in connection with the light: Isa. 49:6 (quoted at Acts 13:47), John 1:4-5, 7-9, 3:19-21; 5:35; 8:12, 9:5; 12:35-36, 46; Acts 9:3, 13:47; 1 Pet 2:9; 1 John 1:5-7, 2:8-10
[157] John 8:12, 9:5 (from: Stern, David H., *Jewish New Testament Commentary*, pp. 181-182)

"His remark was specifically suited to the Feast of *Sukkot* [Tabernacles]; for, according to the Mishna, at the Temple, "there were four golden *menorahs* with four golden bowls at the top of each, and four ladders each leading to a bowl. Four strong young [priests] would climb up with pitchers each holding 9 liters of oil which they would pour into the bowls. From the worn-out drawers and girdles of the [priests] they made wicks, and with them they lit [the *menorahs*]; and there was not a courtyard in Jerusalem that was not lit up by the light of these [festivities]. Pious men and men of good deeds would dance around the menorahs with lit torches in their hands, singing songs and praises, while the Levites played harps, lyres, cymbals, trumpets and innumerable other musical instruments ...." (Sukkah 5:2-4)

"The *Talmud* on this passage says the *menorahs* were 75 feet high (Sukkah 52b) Thus, the water- drawing festival was accompanied by bright lights and

63

- Yeshua is the head of the church which is metaphorically portrayed as His bride.[158] The seven separate candlesticks of the menorah represent the seven churches, or the final church in its entirety.[159]

- Zechariah's candlestick[160] is prophetical of that final church which shall join as one, all the earth under Messiah Yeshua the King, reigning, together with the 144,000 Jews from the Throne of David on Mount Zion[161] in the Synagogue above the tomb of David as the spiritual center and rallying point of all.

- The church fathers also bear witness to the menorah as a symbol of Yeshua.[162]

A Symbolic Representation of the church: As earlier noted, in addressing Yeshua as its eternal head, the church is seen as symbolically represented by the menorah. The seven separate candlesticks now represent the churches or the church in its entirety, no longer just the one entirely Jewish church on Mount Zion that gave birth to all of them.

Now, instead of being restricted to one outward unity and locality, the several churches are mutually independent as to external ceremonies and government, yet one in the unity of the Spirit and headship of Yeshua. I believe that the predominantly "Gentile Christian churches will not realize their unity until the Jewish church (Nazarene Synagogue of

---

dancing—for *Sukkot* is specifically a festival for rejoicing. As before, when the water from Shiloach was being poured and Yeshua used the occasion to invite people to come to Him and drink, now He uses the fact that the feast is accompanied by a blaze of light to announce, "I am the light of the world," adding a promise with implications for both this life and eternity."

[158] Rev. 19:7
[159] Rev. 1:12-13, 20
[160] Zech. 4 (all)

[161] "Then I looked, and there before me was the Lamb, standing on Mount Zion, and with him 144,000 who had his name and his Father's name written on their foreheads." (Rev 14:1) NIV

[162] Among others, Irenaeus draws this conclusion. He writes: "The church announces everywhere the truth and it is the seven branched candlestick which bears on high the light of Christ." See: Bagatti, *The Church of the Circumcision*, page 202

Mount Zion *cum* Messianic Jewish Movement of the World) as the stem, unites all the lamps in one candlestick."[163] [164]

The Messianic Synagogue on Mount Zion was to "shine" because her *"Light* had come."[165] The Gentiles were to come to her *Light.*[166] Her mission as the enlightener of the world was symbolized in the ornamentation of her priesthood. The Urim of the high priest's breastplate signified light, and the name itself is but the plural form of the Hebrew *Or* (light). It stood for revelation, and Thummim for truth.[167]

The Star of David

The six-pointed star that forms the center of the Messianic Seal makes it self-evident that this ancient Jewish symbol was in use for religious purposes at least five centuries earlier than is commonly held by some authorities.[168]

There are many theories about the origin of the Star of David. Some hold that the six-pointed star is an ancient occult symbol. It must be quickly pointed out, however, that the Jewish Star of David always has a top and bottom point lined up vertically. The star, when used in occult rituals, is rotated so that the two side points line up horizontally.[169]

The use of the six-pointed star as a symbol of Judaism, the Jewish people, the State of Israel, and its early King David, has its roots in the ancient Hebrew alphabet in use before and during the time of David. In this alphabet the letter *dalet,* the equivalent of the English "D," was shaped like a triangle. Hence, an ancient, triangular shaped *dalet* was used at both the beginning and the end of the name: DAVID.

When the pagan nations went to war, they many times painted fearsome dragons, snakes or other creatures on the shields of their soldiers. The Israelites chose instead to use the Star of David—two interlaced, equilateral triangles (*dalets*) which were both the first and last

[163] Ibid.
[164] Romans 11:16-24
[165] Isa. 60:1
[166] Isa. 60:3
[167] Pratt, Dwight M., "Light," *International Standard Bible Encyclopedia,* Original Edition 1915, Electronic Database, Biblesoft, 1996
[168] Encyclopedia Judaica, "Magen David," (" ... the Magen David was missing in general use as a religious symbol until the thirteenth century") No 11, page 687
[169] Chamberlin, Rick, *Petah Tikvah Magazine,* Vol. 16, No. 4, Petah Tikvah, Israel

letters of their King's name. Since King David had a well-deserved reputation as a great man of war, this proved to be an excellent and effective symbol for warfare. [170]

Today the *Magen David* (Star of David) is the very embodiment of Zionism, Israel, and Judaism.[171] It is found in every synagogue and it flies proudly as a modern day Star of David on the Israeli flag. As a further commentary on how sacred the Star of David has come to be regarded by religious Jews, young Jewish adults often receive a Star of David charm as a gift to wear around their necks on the occasion of their *Bar/Bat Mitzvah* (confirmation).

From another traditional perspective, held by some in the Church, the points of the Star of David are said to represent the six attributes of God: power, wisdom, majesty, love, mercy and justice. Perhaps then, it isn't too much of a reach to suggest that this symbol might be taken to represent the God of Abraham, Isaac and Jacob, Himself.

Another church tradition holds that the six points of the Star of David signify the six days of the Creation, and that the center of the star represents the seventh day: the Shabbat rest.

Beyond church tradition, there is substantial scriptural support to suggest that the *Magen David* is a symbolic representation of Messiah Yeshua:

- A passage of Messianic prophecy proclaims ... *A star shall come forth from Jacob, and a scepter shall rise from Israel.*"[172]

- Yeshua said of Himself, *I am the root and the offspring of David, the bright morning star.*[173]

- After Yeshua's birth in Bethlehem, the magi arrived from the east in Jerusalem saying, *Where is He who has been born king of the Jews? For we saw His star in the east, and have come to worship*

---

[170] Ibid.
[171] Rev. 12:1 This woman is a "type"of Israel and the twelve stars represent the twelve patriarchs for whom the twelve tribes are named. See: Wilson, Walter L., *Wilson's Dictionary of Bible Types*, "Star," page 432
[172] Num 24:17 (NASV)
[173] Rev. 22:16 (NASV)

Him.[174] I would suggest that what they saw proclaiming the Glory of Yeshua in the morning sky was the Star of David.

- At least one church father wrote that the Star was a symbol of Yeshua.[175]

- Judaism understands this Star (as it is alluded to in Numbers 24:17) to be the Messiah.[176]

- Joseph is commonly seen as a "type" of Yeshua. In his dream, as recorded in Gen. 37:9, Wilson (and others) suggest the meaning is that the eleven stars were the eleven brothers of Joseph, while the sun and the moon represented Joseph's father and mother. This dream is a prophecy, and it was fulfilled in Gen. 42:6, and four times following this. These eleven brothers bowed down to their brother Joseph, just as he had dreamed.[177]

The Fish

There are 34 uses of the Hebrew *dagah* (fish) in the Old Testament and 29 uses of the Greek *ichthus* (fish) in the New Testament. From my

---

[174] Matt. 2:2 (NASV)

[175] Justin Martyr writes, " Another prophet, Isaiah, announces the same thing in other words. A star will rise in Jacob and a flower will sprout on the stalk of Jesse, and the nations will hope in his arm. This bright star which rises, the flower on the stalk of Jesse is the Messiah." See: Bagatti, B., *The Church of the Circumcision*, page 162

[176] (From: Stern, David H., *Jewish New Testament Commentary*, pp. 758-759)

"In the twelfth century, the Ramban (Nachmanides) wrote:

' "There shall step forth a star out of Jacob." Because the Messiah will gather together the dispersed of Israel from all the corners of the earth, Balaam compares him [metaphorically] to a star that passes through the firmament from the ends of heaven, just as it is said about [the Messiah]: 'and behold, there came with the clouds of heaven one like unto a son of man," etc. [Daniel 7:13].'

[177] Wilson, Walter Lewis, *Wilson's Dictionary of Bible Types*, "Star," Grand Rapids: Wm. B. Erdmans Publishing Co., 1957, page, 432

review, I found that none of the verses wherein these 63 uses are made, provided even the slightest hint of direct or indirect scriptural support of the commonly understood notion that the fish is a symbol of Yeshua haMashiach.

There is, however, through several indirect references, an inferential scriptural foundation upon which to conclude that the fish may properly be seen to represent Yeshua in His position as head of the universal church:

- Scripture records two different occasions where Yeshua miraculously multiplied bread and fish in order to feed the crowds that followed Him.[178] It is widely understood that the fish in these instances represents believers in Yeshua (collectively the church) and that His miraculous multiplication in each case is illustrative of potential church growth. Interestingly, *dagah*, the Hebrew feminine form of the word meaning "fish," also is translated as "to multiply, increase, or grow."

- A parallelism is suggested comparing good fish and bad fish with good and evil men, both species of which are caught in nets, then separated. Here again, the reference is straight forward: the fish are compared to people (believers and non-believers in general), the believers having been fished from the net to constitute the Body of Yeshua (the church). [179]

- The church, thus comprised of baptized believers (individually and collectively symbolized by the fish).[180] is euphemistically compared to a "bride,"[181] waiting for her "groom," Yeshua

- Yeshua is the scripturally established head of the church (which is symbolized by the fish).[182]

---

[178] Matt. 14:17, 15:34
[179] Matt 13:47-48
[180] Ps. 45:10-16; Hos. 2:19-20; Isa. 62:5; Matt. 25:1-10; 2Cor. 11:2; Eph 5:32; Rev. 19:7, 21:2, 21:9
[181] As an interesting aside, Jewish brides are immersed in a *mikvah* (analogous to water baptism) as an act of purification just before their wedding ceremonies.
[182] Direct references are: Eph. 1:22-23, 5:23; Col. 1:18. Indirect references are: Matt. 9:15; Heb 13:20; 1Pet 5:4

- From another perspective, Yeshua is present within each believer and therefore, through them and with them, He is present within the church.[183]

It therefore follows that the fish can be seen as a scripturally supported symbol representing: (1) individual believers, (2) believers collectively (individual churches, groups of churches, and all churches seen as the Universal Church or the Universal Body of Christ) and therefore, inferentially, as (3) Yeshua Himself.

The first known written record of the fish as a Christian symbol was made by Clement of Alexandria in about 150 CE, when he suggested to all his readers that they would be well served to include the sign of a fish in their personal seals. Since Clement was a believer, and he didn't find it necessary to expand on why he had made this suggestion, it is easy to infer that the Christian symbolism associated with the fish was by then commonly understood.[184] Indeed, we know from many sources that the symbolic fish was familiar to believers long before the famous Alexandrine was born; in such Roman monuments as the Capella Greca and the Sacrament Chapels of the catacomb of St. Callistus, the fish was depicted as a symbol in the first decades of the second century.

It is most interesting to note that the eight artifacts containing the Messianic Seal, each with the fish as one of its three component symbols, have also been dated to the very beginning of the second century.

In light of the reality of our eight artifacts, each bearing the three-part Messianic Seal, it seems patently obvious that the fish was first used by the Messianic Synagogue on Mount Zion, not as an individual symbol, but as an integral part of a three-part symbol, whose total meaning was considerably different and, if nothing else, at least more inclusive than that of the fish alone.

Referring back to the time when the Nazarenes were forcibly ejected from Israel by other Jews and the Gentile Christian church, and considering as well the ongoing intense campaign by this same Christian church to cleanse itself of all things Jewish, it would also seem patently obvious that the fish was purposefully separated from the other two very Jewish rooted elements (the menorah and the Star of David) before it was, by itself, transported to Rome.

---

[183] John 6:56, 14:20; Rom. 8:10
[184] Hasset, Maurice M., *The Catholic Encyclopedia*, Electronic Version, "Symbolism of the Fish."

Even so, it is very likely that the fish symbol was used by itself as a sign by which early Gentile Christians found and identified one another, especially in times of persecution, such as in Rome when the early believers had to remain hidden in the catacombs, before Constantine's conversion.

I think it also fair to conjecture that Paul, in his various travels to minister to the Gentiles, could have deliberately presented them with the much more simple singular symbol of the fish.

Certainly, none of the Gentiles would have had much understanding of the significance of the two other Jewish elements of the Messianic Seal. Also, the detached fish, consisting of two easily drawn intersecting lines, would have been a far more "user friendly" recognition sign than the much more complex three-part Messianic Seal.

While, as we have seen, there is substantial support in Scripture to legitimatize the fish as a Christian symbol, it seems certain that its great popularity among believers through the centuries arose almost exclusively from the famous acrostic consisting of the initial letters of five Greek words forming the word for fish (Ichthys) which briefly but clearly described the nature of Christ and His claim to the worship of believers: *Iesous Christos Theou Yios Soter,* i.e., Jesus Christ, Son of God, Savior.[185] As seen in *Iesous* (Jesus), "J" is rendered as "I" in Greek, thus the INRI which was placed at the top of His Cross, stands for (I) Jesus (of) (N) Nazareth, (R) Rex (king) (of the) (I) Jews.

I believe, however, it is appropriate to point out that this Greek language acrostic is not scripturally founded. It is, rather, a simple word game with only anecdotal relevance, in a language foreign to the early Jewish believers on Mount Zion whose presumably all Hebrew language writings were at least mostly self-generated.

Even worse, many Christians may yet be unaware that the fish symbol, to which they give credence, has distinctly evil roots.[186]

While this acrostic became widely known and commonly referenced throughout the Gentile Christian church, there is no evidence whatsoever that it ever made its way to the Mount Zion Synagogue, which, in my opinion, it most likely did not.

I would suggest that the fish did not become widely used as a separate symbol until it became popularized in the early Gentile Christian churches outside of Israel, where it had been imported, stripped of the menorah and *Magen David.*

---

[185] Ibid.
[186] The fish was worshipped as the emblem of fecundity; the pagan god Dagon, among the Philistines, half man half fish; also in Assyria.

If the fish as a symbol did not come to the Nazarenes by way of the acrostic, the question is begged: " How did they learn of it, and what, then, did it represent to them that was of sufficient importance for it to be included in their sacred three-part symbol?"

In the end, there is nothing enigmatic here. The Nazarenes had available to them the Gospel According to the Hebrews, (a precursor of the Gospel of Matthew) hand written in Hebrew, and, presumably, other early New Testament references in their sacred library. They surely could have reached the same conclusions suggested above: they, as believers, their Messianic Synagogue, and (by scriptural inference) Yeshua (even if only inferentially), all could be reasonably symbolized by the fish.

The Fourth Symbol: the *Taw*

The *Taw* is really a symbol within a symbol that inarguably appears as the eye of the fish in one of our four artifacts (the "anointing oil stand"), where the head of the fish is visible. While it is not absolutely certain, under magnification, the eye of the fish in the symbol on the "oil dispensing vial" artifact could also originally have been a *Taw*. Now, however, only the vertical and the right horizontal members of what might be a *Taw* remain.

I would suggest that the left horizontal member of the *Taw*, like other areas of the design may have been worn away by time. Or, the less speculative observer might suggest that the eye of the fish in this case is simply a three part drawing of an eye, nothing more. In any event, the unmistakable presence of the *Taw* in the eye of at least one of the artifacts is, I believe, very significant indeed.

As Reuven pointed out, the *Taw* was probably used by the Essenes as a sign meaning salvation.[187] More germane is the near certainty that the Nazarenes regarded the *Taw* as Yeshua's cross.[188] This being the case, it would seem clear that by putting the sign of His cross within the fish symbol, the Nazarenes were affirming the fish as a symbol of Yeshua in His capacity as the head of their synagogue.

---

[187] Schmalz, Reuven E., foregoing historical account, footnote 64, page 30
[188] The church father, "... Origen relates how to assure the meaning of the letter *Taw*, he asked three Jews, among whom one 'who believed in Christ,' who gave him the awaited reply, namely, that the *Taw* symbolised the Cross." See: Bagatti, *The Church from the Circumcision*, page 82. Bagatti later continues: "The Taw for the Christians indicated the salvific cross; with the Jews, on the contrary, it had lost its original meaning and they intentionally omitted it in the anointing of the priests, thus changing the primitive [Essene] tradition. (page 147).

The *Aleph* and the *Taw*

Like Reuven, who discovered the highly significant olive tree "shoots" while yet again pondering the artifacts after he had finished his final editorial polishing, my wife, Donna, just before our publication deadline, was led to excitedly point out yet another seemingly very important aspect of the Seal that we all had previously overlooked. We believe the significance of this latest revelation is such that it must be included.

I invite the reader's attention to the Star of David in the middle of the "Seal." Please note the six points, including the line that intersects each of them, separating them from the rest of the symbol (see below). This resulting six times repeated symbol, which in mathematics, means "not greater than," is also a perfectly rendered *Aleph*, first letter of the ancient Hebrew alphabet.

Yeshua said (in Hebrew, not Greek) "I am the Alpha (*Aleph*) and the Omega (*Taw*), the Beginning and the End, the First and the Last."[189] Thus, I suggest that the Messianic Seal contains yet another indication that it is, with this clear inclusion of both the *Aleph* and the *Taw*, a symbolic representation of Messiah Yeshua, Himself.

Putting the Parts Together

As the circle of those who have beheld the Messianic Seal continues to grow, so do the number of interpretations of its meaning. I pray that this edifying and intensely interesting process will continue until ultimately, out of all this conjecture, there comes a great and wonderful fruition of the many expectations I see implicit in the Lord's purpose for all of this, as the world winds down to His soon second coming.

For my own interpretation which follows, I have established several self imposed ground rules:

---

[189] Rev. 22:13

- Every inferred meaning has been based upon, in order of preference: a direct reference to scripture[190], an inferential reference to scripture, credible, documented history, scholarly analysis, or some combination of any or all of these "yard sticks."

- Speculation, qualified as such and used to enrich any otherwise properly founded inferred meaning, has been included, but pure speculation has not.

- Every inferred meaning has been carefully documented.

- Interpretations are based upon the "Seal" as it was uniformly positioned on each of the artifacts by the Nazarenes who were, presumably, divinely inspired when they did so: The menorah being always at the top, pointing upwards.

---

[190] While there is historical evidence that the Nazarenes had available the "Gospel According to the Hebrews" (which was spoken of as an almost identical precursor of the Gospel of Matthew) no copy of this "first" written gospel has survived. It, along with presumably other later to be canonized New Testament Scriptures, written by various Nazarenes, presumably in Hebrew (or possibly in Greek), were either lost during the exodus of the Nazarenes from Jerusalem, or otherwise later vanished. Even so, looking again to history, we know, with some reasonable assurance, approximately when each of the New Testament books was written, and, in most cases, where they were written and by whom.

Thus, those New Testament writings that were written up to 400 CE by those who were connected to the Mount Zion Synagogue, most likely were available to the Nazarenes for their study and other various contemplation. Included in such writings that thus could have been and, in my opinion, most likely were, available to the Nazarenes were: The Gospels According to Matthew and John; several epistles including: Hebrews, James, 1 and 2 Peter, 1, 2, and 3 John, Jude, and the Revelation. The Lutheran theologian R.C.H. Lenski, in the introduction to his *Interpretation of St. John's Gospel*, writes: "Before the destruction of Jerusalem, between the years 66 and 69, the Apostle John, together with other apostles and disciples of Yeshua, moved to Asia Minor, and these made their headquarters in Ephesus, where Paul had established the most important church of this territory. Here, the Apostle John wrote his Gospel in his old age ... near 80 or 85 [CE]. The three Epistles of John were most likely written after the Gospel, and Revelation last of all." See: Lenski, R.C.H., *The Interpretation of St. John's Gospel*, Minneapolis: Augsburg Publishing House, 1943, page 20. Other commentators agree on the location of Ephesus, but suggest significantly earlier dates, generally around 70 CE as when John wrote these later-to-be-canonized books.

73

My own initial, unstudied reaction, after I first held the artifacts in my own hands, was admittedly well-seasoned with both the excitement of new discovery and the polemics that color the outlook shared by many of my brethren *olim* (immigrants).

I must confess that I have since long struggled and prayerfully sought His guidance on how I should summarize all this in some sort of at once scripturally sound, edifying and reasonable interpretation. At first, I was overwhelmed by all manner of "interesting" ideas and I set out to express them on several different levels of presumed understanding. This approach quickly proved itself, at best, tedious.

There is much wisdom to be found in the adage: "When one jumps into the water and first confronts the alligators, it is difficult to remember that the original objective was to drain the swamp." My "objective" from the outset in this present writing has been to provide an interpretation of the Messianic Seal of the Jerusalem Church from my own perspective as an Israeli Messianic Jew, and in the end, with one modification, this is the approach I have taken. Instead of just one, I offer two iterative interpretations; the first, from what I would presume to be a Nazarene perspective; the second, my own.

How the Nazarenes Themselves Might Have Interpreted the "Seal's" Meaning

Scripture abounds with the concept established by Yeshua: First to the Jew, then to the Gentile.[191] Yeshua was first the Jewish Messiah, even though He was mostly rejected by those to whom He was first given; hence, His later presentation by Paul to the Gentiles in order to make the Jews jealous.[192]

The Messianic Seal, given first as a divine inspiration to the distinctly Messianic Jewish Synagogue on Mount Zion, has reemerged after nearly twenty centuries of suppression, only once again to be given "first to the Jews"—the contemporary Messianic Jewish body in Israel —and only then to the Gentile Christian church, and the world beyond.

As the Nazarenes were inspired to etch and draw the Messianic Seal on our tiny remnant of eight surviving artifacts, and then stood back to behold and contemplate the work of their own hands—I believe they might have seen:

---

[191] Romans 1:16, Matt. 4:23
[192] Romans 11:11

74

In the Menorah:

- The incomprehensible Glory of *YHWH*
- The Light (*phos*) of their Messiah,Yeshua
- By inference, the Holy Spirit who is one with the Father and the Son
- Themselves, as the then extant Body of Messiah, in its central stand
- The Nation of Israel, from national, cultural and social perspectives

In the Six-pointed Star:

- Their promised and come Jewish Messiah, Yeshua[193]
- By inference, the Father and the Holy Spirit
- King David: in the "double *dalets*," and also as made evident by the location of their Messianic Synagogue directly over his tomb, thus proclaiming the fulfillment of Isaiah 11:1.
- The Nation of Israel, from national, cultural and social perspectives, although, to a perhaps lesser degree than they saw Israel in the Menorah

In the Fish:

- Their Messiah,Yeshua, as the spiritual head of their synagogue
- By inference, the Father and the Holy Spirit
- Themselves as individual believers
- Themselves, collectively, as members of the extant Body of Yeshua

---

[193] Fulfillment of the various Messianic prophesies, to include: Gen. 37:9, Num. 24:17, Isa.11:1, etc.

In the *Taw* rendered as the eye of the Fish:

- An affirmation of their understanding of and belief in the salvational power of Yeshua's sacrificial death upon the cross
- A reinforcement of their use of the Fish as an inferred symbol of Yeshua.

In the *Aleph* rendered as each point of the Star of David:

- Together with the *Taw*, another affirmation that the Seal is a symbolic representation of Yeshua, Himself

A Narrative Summary of a Presumed Nazarene Interpretation

Yeshua, the Nazarenes' promised Messiah, sprang out of the stump of Jesse, and through their faith in Him, they founded their Messianic Synagogue directly upon the tomb of David, symbolized as the Star of David in the center of the "Seal."

They, as the first born-again believers, saved individually by Yeshua's sacrifice on the cross, further testify that they have Yeshua dwelling within them. Individually, their salvation through the cross is symbolized by the *Taw* rendered as the eye of the Fish. The *Taw* thus affirms that the symbol of the Fish represents each individual born-again believer, and all of them, collectively, as they together form the very first body of Yeshua, with Yeshua Himself as its head (literally *in* its head as the eye). Thus, Yeshua, Himself is, inferentially, symbolized by the Fish.

Yeshua, as the head of the body, proclaims Himself to be the "Root,"[194] hence the position of the Fish at the bottom of the "Seal," where He, in His capacity as head of the body, and the body itself are symbolically "rooted," with the church thus formed on a biblically strong foundation.[195]

The light stemming from the Menorah, at the very top of the "Seal," symbolizes the unspeakable Glory of *YHWH*, which is one with the Light

---

[194] Rev. 22:16

[195] 1Kings 5:17; Isa. 28:16, Zech. 8:9; Matt. 7:25; Luke 6:48 In Matt. 16:18-19, Yeshua names Simon "Peter" (*Kefa*, meaning "Rock") and then declares His intention to build His church upon this "Rock."

(*phos*) of Yeshua. The symbolic Light of the Menorah reaches ever upward to the source of all *Light*.

Yeshua is also symbolized by the combined presence of the *Aleph* at each point of the Star and the *Taw* in the eye of the fish—" I am the Alpha (*Aleph*) and the Omega, (*Taw*) the Beginning and the End, the First and the Last."

The center stem of the Menorah, another scriptural symbol of the body, terminates in the stand, which forms one of the two superimposed *Dalets* which together form the Star of David.

The Star of David, thus formed, symbolically affirms the rich covenant relationship between themselves and their God which began in the Garden of Eden and continued on through the promises made to David. They are His people and He is their God, the provider all things, the greatest of which is their newly come and now risen Messiah, Yeshua, who, having ascended before their very eyes, has fulfilled all of these covenantal promises.

The Star also provides a conduit through which nourishment flows to the body out of its Jewish roots in the Davidic stump from which it has risen, as it reaches ever upward, through the stem of the Menorah (a continuing representation of the body) to embrace in worship the unspeakable *Light* at the top, itself symbolizing the very Glory of the Triune Godhead.

An Interpretation of the Messianic Seal of the Jerusalem Church from my own Israeli Messianic Jewish Perspective

In the Menorah, I see:

- In the *Light* emanating from the seven individual candlesticks, the ineffable Glory of the Father, the Son and the Holy Spirit, the same *Light* that made Moses' face to glow.

- In the center stem, the body of Messianic Jewish believers, that even today survive as a divinely chosen remnant with an appointed purpose[196] that will continue until Yeshua once again reigns as King from the throne of David on Mount Zion, together with

---

[196]   This divine purpose of the body of Messianic Jews is appointed by many scriptures, a sampling of which includes: Isa. 2:2-5, 11:10, 49:6; Mi. 4:1-2; Matt. 28:19; John 12:32; Acts 13:47

144,000 Messianic Jews.[197] Then at last there will be peace in Israel and throughout the world: *The wolf also shall dwell with the lamb, the leopard shall lie down with the young goat, the calf and the young lion and the fatling together; and a little child shall lead them.*[198]

- In the seven individual candlesticks, the many branches and divisions within both the Gentile Christian church[199] as well as within contemporary Messianic Judaism.

- The very embodiment of the Nation of Israel and the State of Israel of which I am so blessed to be a part, taking in all segments of our people from those who don't yet know the Lord to those who love Him passionately. This is my Land, given to all Jews as an everlasting inheritance, and these are my people, chosen by God for His divine purposes.

In the Star of David I see:

The very substance of my Lord and Savior, Messiah Yeshua, and through Him and in His essence, which is the same, the Father and the Holy Spirit. This symbolic representation of Messiah Yeshua is beautifully reinforced by the multiple *Alephs* in the Star combined with the *Taw* in the eye of the fish: Yeshua said, "I am the *Aleph* and the *Taw* ...."

- My deeply sacred Jewish roots, reaching down, first through the substance of Yeshua, who, as it was prophesied, rose up out of the House of David then proceeding from Him, down through the tunnels of time through David, Jesse, Obed, Boaz, Salmon, Nahshon, Amminadab, Ram, Hezron, Perez, Judah, to Jacob, later named *Israel* by the Word of God, who was the first of the Jews.

---

[197] Rev. 14:1 I would further suggest that the sign that was written on their heads was the *Taw*, the same ancient form of the Hebrew letter that appears as the eye of the Fish in at least one of our artifacts.
[198] Isa. 11:6

[199] Rev. 1:11

- As in the Menorah, here is the very essence of Israel, Judaism, the Nation of Israel and the State of Israel, but from a slightly different perspective, for in the Star I see more of the secular vibrancy of Zionism where in the Menorah, I see things more spiritual than worldly.

In the Fish I see:

- Messiah Yeshua, pointed out to me by my Nazarene predecessors, who, by scribing His cross as the eye of this symbol, seem to be admonishing contemporary Messianic Judaism not to perceive the Fish as an entirely Gentile representation of the Messiah, even when it stands alone, after having been torn asunder from the very Jewish Star of David and Menorah.

- Messiah Yeshua as the head of the church, to include all of its many branches comprised of all believers of all backgrounds and denominations, Jewish and Gentile alike; and, each of these individual believers who comprise the many churches who make up this one universal body of Yeshua.

A Narrative Summary of my Interpretation of the Messianic Seal from an Israeli Messianic Jewish Perspective

Each time I behold the Messianic Seal, my eyes are first instantly directed to the Star of David at its center. For, in my heart, I know that in this symbol of the King rests the very substance and fulfillment of God's incredible plan for the redemption of His people that began in the Garden of Eden and won't end until Yeshua returns to take His rightful place as the King of the Jews in the very place where the Nazarenes were anointed by Him to inaugurate His Body, and where the Bright Morning Star will shine forth once again, illuminating the entire world for the one thousand years He will reign from the throne of David on Mount Zion.

From the Star, my gaze moves naturally down to the cross in the eye of the Fish. And, this transition from Star to Fish is "seamless" because the two symbols are indeed more than just metaphorically of one substance, they are literally cut from the same symbolic cloth—the Fish's tail being also half the Star.

I must confess that I am an oddity among Messianic Jews, in that I am not at all offended by the symbol of the cross, not because of any undue virtue on my part but simply because I came to know Yeshua in the Gentile church and I grew up in a Gentile environment-most of my Messianic Jewish brethren see it as a horrifying reminder of all the hateful and horrific things that have been perpetrated against the Jewish people in the name of Jesus, as so inclusively and poignantly enumerated by Reuven:

"... over a period of nearly 2,000 years, through pogroms, expulsions from occupational guilds, ghettoizations, blood libels, laws forbidding access to higher education or political office, expulsions, burning at the stake, crusades, the slaughter of entire communities, and forced conversions. Capped off with the Holocaust of Annihilation, this calamity was served to the tiny Jewish nation in the name of its own God.[200]"

How it breaks my heart that so many of my brethren can't come to grips with an understanding of what the cross *really* says, and who must instead, struggle to find some less offensive more bearable "cosmetic" way to describe the place where the Son of God died, such as "execution-stake."[201]

Also in the Fish, I see His bride the church, in all of her many branches and divisions, Gentile and Jewish alike—but she is anything but prepared for His second coming. She is torn asunder by division; the promulgator of heretical doctrine—such as "replacement theology;" the ordainer of perversion—significantly more than half of her "shepherds" are even themselves not born again and instead of leading their flocks to eternal life in Yeshua, they guide them either purposefully or through neglect along an ever more crowded pathway into the eternal lake of fire. But, still, in the Fish I see a message of hope, because Yeshua Himself is at its head and in Him all things are possible.

And then, as my very soul cries out in painful intercession for the church, my eyes are gently directed, I am certain, by the healing power of the Holy Spirit, upwards, pausing for a moment of contemplation to "sit" upon the "stump," there to relish in the pervasive Jewishness of God's plan for redemption, symbolized by His glorious Star waiting there on the throne of David for the King's soon return—then, once again, I am on my pathway upwards, recognizing once more the seamless transition from Fish to Star, then from Star to Menorah—to bathe at last in a hint of

---

[200]   Schmalz, Reuven, E., Part One, p. 9
[201]   Stern, David H., "New Testament Commentary," Introduction, page x

the Glorious light of the Godhead, a mere insinuation of the *Light* to come, seen for now in the light of the Menorah as it reaches upwards to the source of all *Light*.

In the end, what I see in the Messianic Seal of the Jerusalem Church is a perfect reflection—a mirror image of the Triune God—Father, Son and Holy Spirit, each present in each of the three separate elements—three made one by the bonding power of the Holy Spirit, yet still three—giving glory unto glory. Amen.

The Contemporary Significance of the Messianic Seal of the Jerusalem Church

In the end, what does all of this mean? Is the incredible multi-faceted testimony of the Messianic Seal to be just another spiritual flower reemerged after 2,000 years of suppression only to bloom for a time unseen and unheard? Surely, this couldn't have been God's intention.

While praying for some special insight regarding the contemporary relevance of the Messianic Seal, I recently attended a meeting of intercessory prayer warriors who gathered together from the northern parts of Israel. I believe that my presence there was a divine appointment—the resounding theme of the meeting, stated again and again by a procession of both Gentile and Messianic Jewish leaders—offered up in praise songs and as the subject of almost every prayer—the theme of this meeting was surely the answer to my quest regarding the contemporary relevance of the Messianic Seal—

Reconciliation and the Breaking Down of Barriers

It seems to me that there were and remain two principal antagonistic detractors from the blessed but perpetually elusive unity which could surely be found as a central theme in many of the very diverse doctrines, practices and traditions of the numerous and greatly varied branches of the universal church, including those of Messianic Judaism.

Yeshua hears and surely must equally delight in the praises rising forth in the soul stirring, rhythmic outpourings of a Black Gospel choir; the haunting melodious and many parted harmonious repetitions of a Gregorian chant, and in the glory of the *Shemah* sung in Hebrew by a Messianic Jewish Congregation.

I would suggest that the purpose of God in presenting us with the Messianic Seal is to show us the error of our ways—to point out through the unavoidable message of unity, implicit in this precious symbol, that there is a way back to His purpose—a way to restore and to break down man-made barriers.

To me, the logical place to begin this work of restoration and the breaking down of barriers is with Messianic Judaism's two historical and continuing antagonists: the Rabbis and the Church.

Reconciliation and the Breaking Down of Barriers from a Jewish (Rabbinical) Perspective

I find it at once deeply saddening yet absolutely fascinating that the Nazarenes, who, during the early decades of the first millennium, up to 135 CE, while they openly proclaimed and worshipped Messiah Yeshua, even doing so in synagogues other than their own, and in spill-over assemblies in the very courts of the Temple, were never-the-less respected and accepted by many non-believing Jews who were later to become their antagonists.

The reason for this abrupt change in the acceptance of the Nazarenes is at once as startling as it is instructive. While at least many of Jerusalem's Jewish establishment were willing to tolerate the Nazarenes' faith in Yeshua's fulfillment of Messianic prophecy, the living hell of Jew against Jew erupted only when the Nazarenes refused to abandon their faith in Yeshua in favor of Rabbi Akiva's messianic substitution of Bar Kochba (Son of the Star). Worse yet, in 135 CE, the Nazarenes refused to join in an open armed revolt against Rome, principally, I presume, because it was launched in the name of one whom they knew to be a false messiah.

To me, it is inexplicable that the rabbis could warmly tolerate the Nazarenes' professed Messiah Yeshua for more than sixty years, and then, seemingly overnight, and for the next nearly 2,000 years, categorically reject any Jew who embraces this same Messiah Yeshua whom they once openly tolerated.

There would seem to be no easy explanation for this rabbinical rejection of the Jewish followers of Yeshua. Certainly, an acceptable explanation cannot be ascribed to the long past and now, for many centuries, irrelevant Nazarene refusal to take up arms in a revolt against Rome. Nor can I find any other plausible explanation. Sadly, I can only observe that this incredibly deep schism between Jew and Jew, who otherwise hold so much in common, continues on today with even greater focus and intensity, and the need for reconciliation cries out unheard, as if in a vacuum.

When a Jew becomes a believer in Yeshua, in rabbinical perceptions, he ceases to be a Jew. In contemporary Israel, the Supreme Court has twice rendered decisions that a Jewish believer in Yeshua is not any longer a Jew; that somehow, during the spiritual process wherein his heart became circumcised, the blood flowing through it no longer carries the DNA of Abraham, Isaac and one or more of the twelve tribes of Jacob (Israel); and somehow, therefore, this now spiritual "born again" Jew is not entitled to be a physical citizen of the State of Israel.[202]

The three-part Messianic Seal of the Jerusalem Church clearly underscores truth, justice and freedom—each a pillar of the Mosaic Law upon which the State of Israel was founded—and the implicit wrong of such a national policy that a Jew, having experienced an entirely spiritual process, has, in so doing, somehow renounced, *de facto*, his right to share in the everlasting spiritual and material inheritance given

---

[202] The Declaration of Independence of the State of Israel, May 14, 1948, states in part: "The State of Israel: will be founded on the principles of freedom, justice and peace envisaged by the prophets of Israel (and) will guarantee freedom of religion, conscience, language, education, and culture."

Sadly, in routinely repeated government practice, those Jews who are in every other way qualified, except that they profess a belief in Yeshua are denied Israeli citizenship. All others (except these "believers" or *notzrim* applicants) are routinely welcomed as full fledged new "olim" citizen/immigrants. Routinely included in their numbers are blatant atheists, secular humanists who fight religious Judaism at every possible opportunity: there are even those Jews who subscribe to the teachings of Buddha, Mohammed and all manner of other cultist theologies and regimens—all welcomed with open arms as new citizens. But, not so Messianic Jews, who, routinely, even meticulously are searched out, and, when discovered, sent packing, perplexed and broken-hearted, back to from whence they tried in vain to answer God's resounding call to: "Come Home!"

Putting the situation into a more statistical perspective, in 1996, according to official Israeli government figures, 71% of all new immigrants that year stated they were Jewish by religion. Therefore, given that any applicant who declared him or herself to be "believer" would have been rejected out of hand as "no longer Jewish" and not included, the other 29% necessarily were either professed adherents to some faith other than Judaism, atheists, humanists, or who somehow managed to convince those taking their applications that their religious beliefs were properly of no one else's concern but their own.

to him by the God of Abraham, Isaac and Jacob; the God, whom, even more than before his spiritual rebirth, he continues to worship and adore.

It would seem much easier for the rabbis to deal with the occasional Jew who (perhaps to their thinking) has gone spiritually berserk on an individual basis, or even with a relative few who could be written off as a renewed "Christian" cult. But, on Mount Zion traditional Judaism was dealing with a major outgrowth from the Essenes, a large and respected segment of their own people. Today, traditional Judaism must deal with the reality of about 4,000 Messianic Jews in Israel and about another 15,000 around the world, a number that may grow, perhaps quickly—the rabbis are understandably shaken at this prospect.

The Messianic Seal, I believe, lends legitimacy to the concept, even demands in the name of righteousness, that Jews remain Jews irrespective of their own innermost private spiritual orientations. Further, it also provides a credible, compelling and convincing basis for the growing, evangelical, pro-Israel part of the church that supports the unifying concept embodied in the Messianic Seal to now be even more supportive than they were before the "Seal" emerged.

What then can be the way to reconciliation and the breaking down of these terrible barriers. Certainly prayer from every quarter should be the foundation of an organized program that I suggest should also include:

- Translation of this present writing into Hebrew and its widest possible dissemination throughout both religious and secular Jewish groups in Israel. Traditional Judaism, I believe, desperately needs to first understand the Messianic Seal's resounding and multi-faceted message of unity and then to accept this message as a basis for reconciliation between the two faiths. This suggested outreach is not intended and must not be perceived as yet another "Christian" evangelistic assault on rabbinical Judaism. Those who would carry this message to the traditional Jewish establishment must find a way to do so that will enable them to first hear, then accept what the Messianic Seal has to say to them, without labeling the effort as "missionary" and rejecting it out of hand. Only God can provide the kind of direction needed, and I believe that all of us who love Him and His people Israel must solicit His intervention through faithful prayer and fasting.

- Repeated public and private broadcasting of a documentary video centered around the story of the Messianic Seal and its message of reconciliation, as set forth in this writing, to as wide an Israeli audience as possible

- Prayerful and material support of the Israeli Messianic congregations by the Gentile Christian church who would be drawn together to orchestrate this campaign of reconciliation and restoration with sensitivity and direction.

Reconciliation and the Breaking Down of Barriers From a Church Perspective

It seems to me there are two quintessential barriers that continue to separate, in general, all Jews from all Gentiles, and, in particular, Messianic Jews from Gentile Christians. The way to reconciliation seems evident: first these two barriers must be clearly identified—then torn down through a mutual campaign of loving outreach, teaching, repentance and forgiveness.

The First Barrier: "Not Guilty," As Charged

While I find it painful to even include the subject in this context, it is difficult to ignore the widely held view shared by many Gentile Christians who, as a matter of doctrine, proclaim that the Jews, single-handedly, killed Christ. This label of "Christ Killer," thus assigned to all Jews, has surely been validated by history as the blindly followed rallying point used by the likes of Adolf Hitler to justify such anti-Semitic tragedies as the Crusades, the Holocaust, etc.

Even before His death, Yeshua seemed to go out of His way to prevent this pernicious barrier from being erected. He made certain, through the power of the Holy Spirit, its author, that the Word would clearly characterize His sacrificial journey to the Cross as first an unavoidable fulfillment of His Father's and His own plan for the world's redemption, a plan to which He willingly submitted Himself;[203] and beyond this entirely willing self sacrifice, that its actual implementation, His Crucifixion, should only be seen as a joint act of both Jews and Gentiles.

---

[203] John 10:17-18

All three synoptic Gospels give the same account: the Sanhedrin, under the supervision of Caiaphas the High Priest, who was a Sadducee, unanimously condemned Yeshua to death, and it was the Gentiles who did the actual killing.[204]

I find it fascinating that only one of the five well-known and highly respected mainstream Gentile church rooted Biblical commentaries I regularly consult, recognizes that the Mark 10 reference is to be interpreted:

"This is the first express statement that the Gentiles would combine with the Jews in His death; the two grand divisions of the human race for whom He died thus taking part in crucifying the Lord of Glory."[205]

The other four commentators, who generally otherwise offer meticulously detailed interpretations, either entirely bypass this monumentally important passage with no comment at all, or instead offer a brief commentary on some irrelevant subject. As representative of the church at large, these commentators seem to be saying by their silence that even the very suggestion Gentiles may have had a hand in Yeshua's physical demise is more than they can bear, much less attempt to explain.

The Second Barrier:

The "De-Judaizing of Christianity"— the Bitter Fruit of Replacement Theology

Let us never forget that the Lord chose Peter (*Kefa*, the rock), not Paul, upon whom to found and build His church. Peter was an apostle to the Jews.[206] Paul was an apostle to the Gentiles. It was to Peter, the Apostle to the Jews, that the Lord gave the keys to the Kingdom.[207] Even the Fish with a *Taw* for an eye, the third member of the Messianic Seal—a picture of the church with Yeshua as its head—it too is etched out on a piece of stone, its own metaphoric rock foundation.

---

[204] Matt. 20:17-19; Mark 10:33; Luke 18:31-33
[205] *Jamieson, Fausset, and Brown Commentary*, Electronic Edition, Biblesoft.

[206] Gal. 2:7,9
[207] Matt. 16:18-19

An ancient rabbinical text affirms:

" 'The land of Israel is found at the center of the world, Jerusalem at the center of the Land of Israel, the sacred place at the center of Jerusalem, the building of the Temple in the center of the sacred place, the Ark of the covenant at the center of the edifice of the Temple; the foundation stone is placed before the Ark of the covenant, the point from which the foundation of the world began.' Abraham lived here and built here the altar on which he was going to immolate Isaac."

"In introducing Peter as the rock of his church, Yeshua therefore thought of a rock well-known to the Jews, one which stood under the Holy of Holies on which God had founded the world; the rock which the Hebrews had identified with Abraham, the fundamental support of [Judaism]. [208]

It seems evident that the Lord intended to found and build His church replete with Jewishness; just as surely as He ordained that Gentiles, having received the *Light* by way of Jews, might be grafted into the same root that "sprouted" Yeshua, their Messiah, out of the stump of Jesse on Mount Zion. For this would be totally consistent with the meticulously detailed plan of redemption set forth by His own Hand, through the power of its author, the Holy Spirit, in the 66 books of the Bible, including His Father's sacred promise to Abraham, Isaac and Jacob, that from their loins would come a great Nation—the promised Messiah and through this great Nation and through its Messiah Yeshua, all the nations of the world would be incredibly blessed.

Surely, if the Lord had wanted to give the church a Gentile foundation and bestow it with a pervasive, entirely Gentile character and Gentile tradition, He would have waited until later, then given the keys to Paul rather than to Peter. But, this isn't what He did—He gave the keys to Peter.

Even so, the Roman Catholic Church continues to proclaim itself as the true and exclusive representative of God's Kingdom on earth—that there is a "union of the Holy Spirit with the Catholic Church His spouse—(thus giving the Church) a divine mission as teacher from Him—a charter as infallible as it is perpetual."[209]

It was this position of exclusivity that apparently gave rise to the Church's intensive de-Judaizing of the Nazarenes and, along with an equally focused rabbinical opposition, was one of the two forces that ultimately led to the disappearance (by 400 CE) of all Nazarene groups,

---

[208] Quoted by: Testa, Emmanuel, *The Faith of the Mother Church*, page 114
[209] "Rome's Challenge," *The Catholic Mirror*, March 1998, page 10

along with their writings and all but a relatively few examples of their sacred three-part symbol.

Some of the impact of the Roman Church's continuing exclusivity position has spilled over into contemporary situations that directly impact Israel:

- It is not inconsistent with the Church's view concerning its leadership of God's Kingdom on earth, and its accompanying doctrine that it has thus replaced biblical Israel, for any thinking Israeli to give more than passing attention to the continuing media reports that the Vatican ultimately seeks to gain political control over Jerusalem. Moreover, for a reborn State of Israel to have Jerusalem negates the Church's claim.[210]

- While it may seem surprising to some, it was widely reported at the time by the media, that Israel's former Prime Minister Shimon Peres made a written deal with the Vatican which essentially would have turned Jerusalem into an international city overseen by the Holy See."[211] Peres, soon after he thus offered up Jerusalem, lost the premiership to Benjamin Netanyahu by a razor thin margin.

Unhappily, the Roman Church does not stand alone in this doctrinal notion that suggests that all organized Christendom; i.e., the universal Gentile Christian church, has somehow replaced biblical Israel. Many, Protestant groups also hold to at least some sense of this "replacement" theology.

As I have earlier suggested, I believe that the roots of disunity between the Gentile Christian church and relatively minuscule Messianic Judiasm are the hermeneutical variances in their interpretation of certain key Scriptures regarding the continuance of the Torah's teachings as they apply to Messianic Jews and as they do not apply to the Gentile Christian church.

Having thus outlined the problem—where again is the road leading to its solution through reconciliation and the breaking down of barriers?

I would again suggest a concerted, organized, centrally controlled, church-wide, cross- denominational program. Such a program would be

---

[210] Bible Students Congregation of New Brunswick, "After Cuba—where will the Pope go next? —Jerusalem?" February, 1998
[211] "The Vatican's Jerusalem Agenda," *Israel Resource Review*, 22 September, 1997, page 4

organized and led by the Gentile Christian church itself, with an agenda to attack replacement theology head on—using as its text the glorious message of multi-faceted unity implicit in the Messianic Seal.

This challenge may seem too big for man, but it certainly isn't too big for God. I would include in this program, as in the parallel effort directed towards the rabbis, wide distribution of the current writing, as well as wide showings of a documentary video.

In Summary

I am deeply convicted that the Lord brought forth the Messianic Seal of the Jerusalem Church at this time of His choosing. He did so, I believe, as a means to initiate a great cleansing of His church to prepare her for His soon second coming.

As I have endeavored to point out, these barriers will not easily come down: they have seemingly become the very foundation of our thinking over the entire history of the church from the time of its beginnings on Mount Zion.

As a starting point, I believe that the Messianic Seal's wonderful, compelling and pervasive message of *unity* must be etched into the circumcised heart of every born again member of the body—Gentile and Jewish alike. This can only be done by God Himself. We, individually and collectively, as His waiting bride, must first yield ourselves to this purpose of restoration. Then recognizing that only He can break down the barriers, we can trust in Him, knowing that He will.

As a part of this yielding, we must first commit ourselves to a better understanding of what He has already given us in His Word regarding the relationship He has ordained between all Jews—His Nazarenes, contemporary Messianic Judaism, "religious" Jews, and secular Jews alike vis-à-vis all of the many branches of the universal Gentile Christian church.

This is what His Word tells us:

He chose His Jewish people for His own special purposes and He gave them the Land of Israel as their everlasting inheritance:

And God said to him, "Your name is Jacob; your name shall not be called Jacob anymore, but Israel shall be your name." So He called his name Israel. Also God said to him: "I am God Almighty. Be fruitful and multiply; a nation and a company of nations shall proceed from you, and kings shall

89

come from your body ."The land which I gave Abraham and Isaac I give to you; and to your descendants after you I give this land." (Gen 35:10-12)

Biblical Israel has not been replaced by the church, a truth which is clearly proclaimed in the Old Covenant:

Thus says the LORD, who gives the sun for a light by day, the ordinances of the moon and the stars for a light by night, who disturbs the sea, and its waves roar (The LORD of hosts is His name): "If those ordinances depart from before Me, says the LORD, then the seed of Israel shall also cease from being a nation before Me forever. "Thus says the LORD: "If heaven above can be measured, and the foundations of the earth searched out beneath, I will also cast off all the seed of Israel for all that they have done, says the LORD. (Jer. 31:35-37)

This same truth regarding the continuance of biblical Israel is clearly proclaimed in the New Covenant:

Then I looked, and behold, a Lamb standing on Mount Zion, and with Him one hundred and forty-four thousand, having His Father's name written on their foreheads. (Rev. 14:1)

Also she (the New Jerusalem) *had a great and high wall with twelve gates, and twelve angels at the gates, and names written on them, which are the names of the twelve tribes of the children of Israel.* (Rev. 21:12)

Now the wall of the city had twelve foundations, and on them were the names of the twelve (Jewish) *apostles of the Lamb.* (Rev. 21:14)

He gave His Jewish people a responsibility to promulgate His truth to the Gentiles, not the other way around as is so commonly misunderstood:

"And now the LORD says, who formed Me from the womb to be His Servant, to bring Jacob back to Him, so that Israel is gathered to Him (for I shall be glorious in the eyes of the LORD, and My God shall be My strength), Indeed He says, 'It is too small a thing that You should be My Servant to raise up the tribes of Jacob, and to restore the preserved ones of Israel; I will also give You as a light to the Gentiles, that You should be My salvation to the ends of the earth.'" (Isa. 49:5-6)

The Jewish people, through the grace and protection of their Creator, as ordained in His Word, have an incredible resilience. Despite the persecution that has traumatized their entire history, a remnant has somehow, held safe in the very hand of God, managed to survive for yet another day to continue boldly on towards their divinely ordained destiny.

I believe The Messianic Seal of the Jerusalem Church has enjoyed a similar divine protection. Having been stripped of its decidedly Jewish Menorah and Star of David, it has undergone a kind of holocaust of its very own. Even so, like the early Jewish believers whose holy hands first crafted it, a remnant of the Messianic Seal has miraculously once again been resurrected from its nearly 2,000 year burial on Mount Zion. Now, having been so restored to renewed life, it offers a message of *unity* to even those who have been its perpetual antagonists. In the end, we as Messianic Jews, reach out to our Gentile brothers in love and with outstretched arms—come and take our great gift, given to us by the Creator of the universe—the Messianic Seal of the Jerusalem Church.

Then come with us, with the barriers at last torn down and basking in the loving-kindness He always intended we should have between us— come, let us go together to meet Him in the clouds.

"Thus says the LORD of hosts, 'In those days ten men from all the nations will grasp the garment of a Jew saying, "Let us go with you, for we have heard that God is with you."'" [212]

Zechariah 8:23 (NASV)

After Word

I cannot find words to express the awe, gratitude, praise and joy that have truly become the crown of my life through all this. Never before have I really understood what it meant to be Jewish—so much of my life I struggled—trying to be absorbed into the Gentile world—just another one of the faithful sitting in a pew each Sunday morning—happy to be pretending that I was indistinguishable from the rest—lost in the vacuum of the universal church. I used to think: Why in God's name would anyone really want to be Jewish?? Now I know what a distinction being Jewish really is—not just something to worry about when the next Adolf comes around in the form of a Yassar or a Saddam. Now, by the grace of God, I know who and what I am—and I am so at peace with myself and my Maker and the world around me—The Messianic Seal of the Jerusalem Church has spoken volumes to my soul—I am so grateful, so incredibly blessed.

R.R.F.

Tiberias, Israel
April 21, 1999: By His Grace, and by His Hand,
the 51st Anniversary of the founding of the State of Israel

Bibliography

Bacchiocchi, Samuele
> *From Sabbath to Sunday*. Rome: The Pontifical Gregorian University
> Press, 1977

Bagatti, Bellarmino, O.F.M.
> *The Church from the Circumcision*. Jerusalem: Franciscan Printing
> Press, 1984

Bagatti, Bellarmino, O.F.M.
> *The Church from the Gentiles in Palestine*. Jerusalem: Franciscan
> Printing Press, 1984

Baigent, Michael (and) Leigh, Richard
> *The Dead Sea Scrolls Deception*. London: Jonathan Cape, 1991

Barton, George A.
> *Archeology and the Bible*. Philadelphia: American Sunday School
> Union, 1944

Brown, Francis (and) Driver, S.R. (and) Briggs, C.A.
> *Hebrew and English Lexicon of the Old Testament*. London: Oxford
> Press, 1951

Bruce, F.F.
> *New Testament History*. New York: Doubleday, 1980

Chadwick, Henry
> *The Early Church*. London: Penguin Books, 1967

Charlesworth, James H. (Editor)
> *The Old Testament Pseudepigrapha* (Volumes 1 and 2). New York:
> Doubleday, 1983

Cohen, Rabbi Bruce L.
  Why Messianic Judaism? (A Position Paper): Congregation Beth El
  of Manhattan, New York

Concordant Publishing Concern
  Concordant Greek Text. Canyon County, California, 1975

Davidson, Benjamin
  The Analytical Hebrew and Chaldee Lexicon. Grand Rapids:
  Zondervan, 1970

Dugger, A. N.
  A History of True Religion. Jerusalem: Mount Zion Reporter Press,
  1972

Dugger, A.N.
  Daniel and Revelation. Jerusalem: Mount Zion Reporter Press, 1977

Eisenman, Robert
  James the Brother of Jesus. New York: Penguin Books, 1997

Encyclopedia Britannica, Inc.
  The New Encyclopedia Britannica, Fifteeth Edition. Chicago:
  University of Chicago, 1986

Flusser, David
  Judaism and the Origins of Christianity. Jerusalem: The Magnes
  Press, Hebrew University, 1988

Garraty, John A. (and) Gay, Peter
  The Columbia History of the World.. New York: Harper & Row, 1981

Green, J.P. Sr.
  The Interlinear Bible, Hebrew-Greek-English. Boston: Hendrickson
  Publishers, 1986

Harper & Row
  The Nag Hammadi Library in English. Edited by J.M. Robinson, New York:. 1977, 1988

Hislop, Alexander
  The Two Babylons. New York: Loizeaux Brothers, 1959

Juster, Daniel
  Jewish Roots. Gaithersburg, Maryland: DAVAR Publishing Co., 1986

Keter Publishing
  Encyclopedia Judaica. Jerusalem: Keter Publishing, 1982

Korin Publishers
  The Jerusalem Bible. Jerusalem: Korin Publishers, 1980

Latourette, Kenneth Scott
  A History of Christianity. New York: Harper & Row, 1953

Mancini, Ignazio, O.F.M.
  Archeological Discoveries Relative to the Judeo-Christians - Historical Survey, Jerusalem: Franciscan Printing Press, 1984

McGrath, Alister E.
  Christian Theology. Oxford: Blackwell Publishers, 1994

Oxford University Press
  The New Oxford Annotated Apocrypha. New York: Oxford University Press, 1991

Painter, John
  Just James, The Brother of Jesus in History and Tradition. Columbia: University of South Carolina Press, 1997

Parrinder, Geoffery
  Man and His Gods. London: Hamlyn Publishers, 1971

Pritz, Ray A.
    Nazarene Jewish Christianity. Jerusalem: The Magnes Press, E.J. Brill, 1988

Schonfield, Hugh
    The Pentecost Revolution. Chicago: Element Books, 1985

Schonfield, Hugh
    The Essene Odyssey: Element Books, 1984

Stern, David H.
    Jewish New Testament Commentary. Clarksville, Maryland: Jewish New Testament Publications, Inc. , 1990

Stern, David H.
    Messianic Jewish Manifesto. Jerusalem, Israel: Jewish New Testament Publications, Inc., 1988

Terry, Milton S.
    Biblical Hermeneutics. Grand Rapids, Michigan: Zondervan, 1974

Testa, Emmanuel
    The Faith of the Mother Church. Jerusalem: Franciscan Printing Press, 1992

Tout, T.F.
    The Empire and the Papacy. London: Rivington's Publishers, 1924

Wescott & Hort
    The New Testament in Greek. New York: Macmillan, 1948

Wright, George E. (and) Filson, Flyd V.
    The Westminster Historical Atlas to the Bible. London: Westminster Press, 1945

Whiston, William
    The Works of Josephus. Boston: HendriksonPublishers, 1987

Vermes G.
   The Dead Sea Scrolls in English. London: Penguin, 1987

Yadin, Yigael
   Masada. London: Sphere Books, 1966

Yadin, Yigael
   The Temple Scroll. London: Weidenfeld and Nicolson, 1985

YHWH 10-2*,
THE TEMPLE AT LEON Topol 7S 10-1, 2 8-6,
ZADOKITES & ESSENES - 12 I
Intertestimental books had Essene authorship 14-5
Paul & the Essenes 13-4
The usurpation of the seat of David 14-5
NAZARENES 15 B, 33
John 16-8
Mandeans- Johns present Nazarene movement 17
Essenes called Themselves the Way, etc, 18-9
Davids TOMB (Church - Upper Room) 19-20, 22, 31-3, 36, 44-0*, 76-7
First Jerusalem Council in David's tomb 20-1
Eusebius, 13-22
Sadducees were the usurpers or wicked priests 22-4
Josephus 24-7
Zadok - 25-7*
Essene eschatology 26-7, 29
The Zealots were Essene 26
The Damascus document hints at one Messiah 27
Yeshua overode all priesthoods 28*
The Church tried to distance itself from the Jews 30
The seals meaning 30-2
Magen David 30-1
mikvahs 32-4
First Church 32-4
The Lamina 31-4
The oil marble brick - its age 34-5
why the seal remained hidden 34-8
Writers against the Nazarenes 37-9
Paganizing the faith 37-8
Celebrating the Feasts 37-0
The Nazarenes are crucified 40 97
Peters' tomb found in Jerusalem 4/